The Black Archive #21

HEAVEN SENT

By Kara Dennison

Published July 2018 by Obverse Books

Cover Design © Cody Schell

Text © Kara Dennison, 2018

Range Editors: Philip Purser-Hallard, Paul Simpson

Kara would like to thank:

Ginger Hoesly for her cheerleading and funny gifs, and everyone involved in making such a stunning episode.

To my grandfather Charlie and my uncle Emile – the two men who taught (and still teach) me to reach for the stars, no matter what stands in the way.

Also Available

The Black Archive #1: Rose by Jon Arnold

The Black Archive #2: The Massacre by James Cooray Smith

The Black Archive #3: The Ambassadors of Death by LM Myles

The Black Archive #4: Dark Water / Death in Heaven by Philip Purser-Hallard

The Black Archive #5: Image of the Fendahl by Simon Bucher-Jones

The Black Archive #6: Ghost Light by Jonathan Dennis

The Black Archive #7: The Mind Robber by Andrew Hickey

The Black Archive #8: Black Orchid by Ian Millsted

The Black Archive #9: The God Complex by Paul Driscoll

The Black Archive #10: Scream of the Shalka by Jon Arnold

The Black Archive #11: The Evil of the Daleks by Simon Guerrier

The Black Archive #12: Pyramids of Mars by Kate Orman

The Black Archive #13: Human Nature / The Family of Blood by Philip Purser-Hallard and Naomi Jacobs

The Black Archive #14: The Ultimate Foe by James Cooray Smith

The Black Archive #15: Full Circle by John Toon

The Black Archive #16: Carnival of Monsters by Ian Potter

The Black Archive #17: The Impossible Planet / The Satan Pit by Simon Bucher-Jones

The Black Archive #18: Marco Polo by Dene October

The Black Archive #19: The Eleventh Hour by Jon Arnold

The Black Archive #20: Face the Raven by Sarah Groenewegen

CONTENTS

Overview

Synopsis

Introduction

Chapter 1: A Bespoke Torture Chamber

Chapter 2: The Final Nightmare

Chapter 3: The Net Tightens

Chapter 4: Doctor Who?

Chapter 5: Endless Twelve

Chapter 6: Final Thoughts

Bibliography

Biography

OVERVIEW

Serial Title: *Heaven Sent*

Writer: Steven Moffat

Director: Rachel Talalay

Original UK Transmission Date: 28 November 2015

Running Time: 54m 04s

UK Viewing Figures: 6.2 million

Regular Cast: Peter Capaldi (The Doctor), Jenna Coleman (Clara)

Guest Cast: Jami Reid-Quarrell (Veil)

Antagonists: The Veil, the Time Lords

Sequels: *Hell Bent* (TV, 2015)

Responses:

'Watching it play out is an experience, haunting and triumphant, unlike any **Doctor Who** has offered before.'

[Kelly Connolly, *Entertainment Weekly Online*]

'This episode was gold dust for fans of Moffat's fanbait mysteries, which, I uncharitably feel, are beginning to take on a slightly mechanistic air, like the scriptwriter equivalent of search-engine optimisation.'

[Tim Martin, *Daily Telegraph Online*]

SYNOPSIS

(**Clara** is dead and **the Doctor** is betrayed. He has handed his Confession Dial – the repository for a Time Lord's last will and testament – to the immortal **Ashildr**, aka 'Me', and been teleported into the custody of unknown enemies[1].)

In a chamber in a deserted castle, a dying hand activates a teleporter. Its owner crumbles to dust as the Doctor appears, furious and defiant. From the moment he arrives, he is hunted by **the Veil**, a terrifying shrouded creature unearthed from his childhood nightmares. He finds that words of self-revelation temporarily halt its pursuit and cause the building's labyrinthine architecture to rearrange itself. He comes to realise that the castle has been purpose-built to extract a confession from him.

By luring his shambling nemesis to one extreme of the castle, he gains himself periods of time to explore. He discovers a bedroom in which a portrait of Clara hangs; a room where clothes identical to his own wait on a drying rack; a garden where a cryptic message has been buried, directing him to Room 12; and the ocean serving as the castle's moat, where a colossal pile of skulls has accumulated. He observes a tendency (though apparently not a universal one) for the rooms to revert to their original condition after he leaves.

In the teleport chamber, he discovers the word 'BIRD' scrawled in the dust, and his predecessor's skull. He carries this up a tower, where he observes from the stars' positions that 7,000 years have inexplicably passed. He finds the door to Room 12 walled shut.

---

[1] *Face the Raven* (2015).

7

As the Veil approaches, he admits that he knows the identity of the 'Hybrid' foretold in apocalyptic Gallifreyan legend. This changes the castle's structure again allowing access to Room 12 (and incidentally tipping the skull into the moat). In it is a 20-foot-thick wall, harder than diamond, inscribed with the word 'HOME'. He remembers the meaning of 'BIRD', and the true and terrible nature of his situation.

In despair, he retreats into a memory of the TARDIS console room, where he contemplates surrendering to his inquisitors until a vision of Clara urges him to continue. Returning to reality, he painfully punches the wall and begins to tell the Veil a story, until the creature catches up with him and lethally touches him.

In his death throes he crawls agonisingly back to the teleport chamber, which has reset itself – including restoring the data in the teleporter's buffer which first enabled it to embody him. By burning away the energy of his own body, he is able to activate the teleport. He laboriously scrawls the word 'BIRD' before crumbling to dust. Moments later the Doctor appears, as furious and defiant as before.

This cycle repeats itself, and continues for a very long time. In each iteration the prisoner lands a few punches at the wall, eroding it with geological slowness while he tells the story, narrated by a shepherd boy in a Grimm fairytale, of a bird that over aeons wore down a mountain. It takes him billions of years to break through the wall.

He arrives through a portal on Gallifrey, and sees that he has been imprisoned in the Confession Dial. Notifying the **Time Lords** of his arrival, he finally confesses that the Hybrid 'is Me.'[2]

---

[2] Capitalisation as in the script (Moffat, Steven, '**Doctor Who** Series 9 Episode 12 *Heaven Sent*: Blue Amendments', p67.)

INTRODUCTION

Few episodes of **Doctor Who**, be it in the 20th or 21st century, have stirred quite as much reaction as *Heaven Sent* (2015). Daring for being a single-hander, daring as a metaphor for grief, daring visually and psychologically: it's no wonder that it went on to win a variety of awards, and be nominated and shortlisted for more.

The concept of the story itself – an ever-looping timeline – has been explored over and over in both Western and Eastern entertainment. Stephen King's **Dark Tower** series and short piece 'That Feeling, You Can Only Say What It Is in French' reflect his personal motto that 'Hell is repetition'[3]. The 2016 film adaptation of *Dr Strange* (carrying with it some *Heaven Sent* vibes) used the concept of repetition as torture in rather an unexpected way. And *Groundhog Day* (1993), well, goes without saying. That film alone, while not the beginning of the use of the trope by any means, comes to mind in contemporary uses of it, especially within geek and genre entertainment – either via deliberate reference, or by virtue of the film's cultural spread.

This timeline, this rut, is examined as a Hell by the Doctor himself during the episode, and as a cycle of grief by everyone from scriptwriter Steven Moffat all the way down to yours truly. It's a powerful metaphor for what our lives become when we lose someone dear to us, and that symbolism can and should never be forgotten.

---

[3] King, Stephen, endnotes to 'That Feeling, You Can Only Say What It Is in French', *The New Yorker* Summer Fiction issue, 22 and 29 June 1998.

However...

With all the attention given to these metaphors for the viewer and their own life experience, it can be easy to overlook just how much this episode means for the Doctor – with regards to the 12th Doctor as an isolated portrayal, the Doctor himself as a character of more than half a century's standing, and the 'character' of the Doctor that our anonymous protagonist created for himself.

What we have here, from a symbolic and scriptwriting standpoint, is a textbook example of a character development episode. Everything from the architecture of the castle to the clothing the Doctor appears in after *Face the Raven* (2015) feeds into what is, in essence, an hour-long lesson (for the Doctor and for us) on who and what the Doctor is and what happens when that character's evolution is on the table. Just as the castle is the Doctor's bespoke torture chamber, the episode itself is the Doctor's bespoke character development playing field. Every turn, every plot point, every **room** simply adds fuel to this.

The episode takes visual cues from everything from German expressionism to *Citizen Kane* (1941) to director Rachel Talalay's own work in the **Nightmare on Elm Street** franchise. Put together, these visuals – as well as deep-seated symbolism in the Jungian tradition – build what is probably the clearest look we've had since 1963 at the psyche of the individual who has chosen to give himself the name of 'Doctor.'

Was it intentional? Were we meant to have this very clear Doctor 101 lesson? Or is it a by-product of the storytelling? Rather pleasingly, it doesn't matter – whether Moffat intended it or not, it's there for us to explore and to poke at, and gives us an impressive jumping-off point into the fall-out that occurs in *Hell Bent* (2015).

Most of all, it gives us a chance to see what the Doctor – as a metatextual character – does when cornered into such a thing. We know our hero, and we know that he does not like being told what to do[4]. What happens, then, when his very TV show places him in a setting that is traditional and peculiar to growth and development? Considering this iteration of the Doctor is one heavily about exploring the nature of the character – from his early questioning of his own morality[5] to his swan song consisting largely of a list of what being the Doctor means[6] – we are in for at least some answers. But for a series 9 12th Doctor, during his loss of Clara and prior to much of his later education, it's going to be just as rough on his own terms as anything he's done up to this point.

The Doctor – or rather, the person who calls himself 'the Doctor' – is a force to be reckoned with. And whether it's Time Lords wanting answers to an age-old prophecy or a writer demanding catharsis after the loss of a companion, the Doctor will rebel. Even if that means four and a half billion years of punching a wall[7].

---

[4] Clara as his 'boss' in Series 8 to 9 seems to contradict this, but even that drift from his headstrong nature feeds into this discussion.
[5] *Deep Breath* (2014).
[6] *Twice Upon a Time* (2017).
[7] The highest number mentioned in *Heaven Sent* itself is 'two billion years', but *Hell Bent* refers three times to 'four and a half billion years', which seems to be the definitive figure.

CHAPTER 1: A BESPOKE TORTURE CHAMBER

The wonderful thing about *Heaven Sent* is that it's not a stretch to analyse, or even to **want** to analyse – being informed that we're about to watch Peter Capaldi do a one-man show in a murder castle pretty much screams, 'Please deconstruct this.' From the previews it is clear that there will be a great deal of symbolism, and it's probably going to tell us something very important indeed before we go in for the final push of series 9.

It's also the literal centrepiece of a three-parter in a series full of two-parters. While the name pairing continues the theme begun with *The Magician's Apprentice / The Witch's Familiar* (2015), this is the keystone of the triptych created by *Face the Raven* on one side and *Hell Bent* on the other – the central piece that defines the decisions made after the former and sets the stage for the fall the Doctor takes in the latter.

We're given our answers to the riddle of *Heaven Sent* as soon as the Doctor punches his way out of the Confession Dial: his bespoke puzzle box is as much a confessional literally as it is symbolically. While its function is repurposed by the Time Lords for their own ends within the scope of series 9's story arc, its original purpose is served when it comes to the viewers' engagement with the Doctor (and, theoretically, the Doctor's engagement with himself). We, the viewer, do get a handful of straight answers – perhaps not as many as we'd like just yet, but we do get some insight. But even though he notes that he's 'nothing without an audience,'[8] this is very much his

---

[8] All quotations from *Heaven Sent* unless otherwise noted.

own journey; and how (or if) he chooses to make it is just as telling as the blatant truths he blurts out when attempting to escape the Veil.

There are no attempts made to shy away from or 'vague up' the purpose of the castle, or the episode, at all. Yes, the purpose becomes clearer on repeat viewings. But even the opening hands the point to us: soul-searching. The manual on the castle wall (skimmed over visually and elaborated on by the Doctor in monologue) even lays out why we're all here:

> 'As you come into this world, something else is also born.
> You begin your life and it begins a journey.
> Towards you.
> Wherever you go,
> Whatever path you take,
> It will follow.
> You will notice a second shadow next to yours.'

Technically, of course, this is his rule book for the castle – for dealing with the Veil, specifically. But symbolically speaking, we're being told: this is an episode of self-exploration, of moving forward, of acceptance of parts of oneself one would prefer to leave unaddressed. Bluntly, on this week's very special **Doctor Who**, we will be getting character development.

And between the invocation of the Shadow and the use of an entire multilevel building as the Doctor's stage for self-discovery, we're already firmly in Jungian space.

Jung's House

In the 1963 English translation of *Memories, Dreams, Reflections* (1962), Carl Jung recounts the first dream that led him to outline his concept of houses as symbolic of the human psyche. He began on the top floor of what he knew to be 'his' house, working downward floor by floor. As he descended, the decor of the rooms he passed through moved back in time stylistically, until he came upon the bottom floor, which he describes as 'a low cave cut into the rock':

> 'Thick dust lay on the floor, and in the dust were scattered bones and broken pottery, like remains of a primitive culture. I discovered two human skulls, obviously very old and half disintegrated.'[9]

This seems to be, if we subtract one skull, an almost match-for-match description of the chamber the Doctor finds himself in when he comes in through the 'teleporter.' Whether this is a specific invocation of Jung's house dream in addition to the other purposes it serves, we can't know. It's almost certainly more happy happenstance than the first notch on a decoder ring, but it gets us there[10].

Jung's dream is a very straightforward one when it comes to building the basics of his concept. He starts at the top, the conscious mind and higher reason, and descends downward until he reaches the very primal: the subconscious. In this sense, the positioning of rooms and venues in a house or building is just as important as their actual

---

[9] Jung, Carl, *Memories, Dreams, Reflections,* p159.
[10] Besides, 'happy happenstance' is often the name of the game when it comes to discovering symbolism along Jungian lines.

function – the higher up they are, the closer to the conscious mind, logic, and reason they are; the farther down they are, the deeper, more subconscious, and more primal the events and things therein will be.

This method of interpretation is most readily useful for dreams – but the imagery carries through in film and literature, too. Any work where we see a character who is inextricably linked to a building in some way, especially if points are made of their movement through very specific rooms in said building, is prime for this interpretation. A masterclass in this method of interpretation prior to *Heaven Sent* is the 1995 film *Jumanji*, in which a boy must grow up and confront his father-figure while various rooms of his house are overtaken by jungle animals.

Similarly, we see a plot that takes its structure from a player's movement across a 'board' of sorts, from room to room, and the room changing with the choices and actions of that player. *Heaven Sent* is, whether deliberately or accidentally, a delve back into Jung's house imagery.

One of the main problems with analysing the castle from a Jungian aspect is, unfortunately, that by its very nature we don't know exactly where all of the rooms are. We know that the Doctor starts out relatively high up, as he takes an impressive tumble out of the window. We know that he does go to the very top of the castle to observe the stars. We can deduce that the garden and the moat are, based purely on common sense, the lowest venues in the castle – at least until we get to Room 12, which has a distinct subterranean aesthetic to it. Beyond that, the castle shifts and rearranges whenever the Doctor makes a confession. (This aspect is extremely important on its own, but more on that later.) Thus, the ever-shifting nature of the castle precludes that aspect of analysis from a large portion of what we're here to discuss.

Bear in mind, though, that we are working with the 12th Doctor: a character who is outwardly quite prickly and antisocial to start with, but who is ultimately the most vulnerable Doctor yet seen onscreen. Even in our regular dealings with him, we'll see spans of higher logic crumble suddenly under an unexpected voicing of a very deep, very personal fear of loss. To that end, we don't necessarily lose anything by missing that one aspect of the analysis – it's certainly not all that different from watching this Doctor in action on a regular basis. Just as we can't always be sure whether the Doctor is on a high or low floor of the castle in *Heaven Sent*, we can't always be sure from episode to episode whether he will hit us with a thought right from his hearts, or once again protest too much. Room positioning will be addressed where it's clear, but once we begin to lose track of the path taken through the castle it'll have to fall by the wayside.

So, the Doctor's movement through the castle is not like Jung's direct descent: it's not a straight shot down to the subconscious, picking things up along the way. Rather, it's staggered, going from room to room, exploring what is available until his actions open other rooms. It's a journey to a very specific destination, though the Doctor and the Time Lords have very different ideas about what that destination is and how he's meant to get there.

Dust and Skulls

To start at the beginning – the beginning of the story, the episode, the loop, whatever – we find the Doctor in the castle's teleport chamber. We won't actually see much of this room until his later trips through it, so we can only start with what he sees: the aforementioned layer of dust. The immediate reminder of death, in more ways than he can readily fathom at this stage of proceedings. For now, the reminder of Clara's death. That is, after all, why he's here, at least from a story standpoint: to come to terms with the concept of mortality. But a near-immortal alien who has already survived multiple 'permanent' scrapes with death[11] is beyond needing introspection over his own eventual end. Bear in mind, in a few moments we'll see that he's more than ready to admit he fears his own death. He doesn't need a huge amount of help admitting that. The 'death' we see here, depicted throughout the episode in all its forms, is the death of others, the death of friendships, the death of his 'normal'. Quite simply, loss.

It's interesting to note that the brusquer, Occam's Razor Doctor who was perfectly willing to sacrifice a dead man walking without so much as an 'I'm so, so sorry'[12] is the one who began more and more to genuinely be affected by the deaths of those who travel with him. Which is not to say he never was affected – he tends to be – but to have him express the fear of this loss so regularly and so fully without it being a variant on the 'Lonely God' lament heard during the 10th Doctor's tenure is something of a rarity.

And yet the Doctor steps out ready to fight, holding what we'll soon know to be the remnants of his own failure as he declares that he will not ever stop. The context of this room isn't clear to us yet, and

---

[11] The 11th Doctor was at the forefront of the most recent of these: first, Lake Silencio in the first half of series 7, then the subverted end of his regeneration cycle in *The Time of the Doctor* (2013).
[12] *Into the Dalek*.

certainly not to him. We will revisit it later, when he does.

Private Quarters

From a first encounter with the rules, to a first look at himself up high (in other words, we've not delved very deep, but we've also only just got here), to a first encounter with the Veil, and into the next room: a bedroom. Rather bluntly, according to the screenplay, the Doctor's bedroom[13].

It can be extremely tempting in analysis like this to take a room at face value.,. Simply put, the bedroom is where one finds the things and people closest to one's heart(s). There's little to no shock in seeing a portrait of Clara hanging on the wall; he has, after all, spent an entire series or two shunning any contact save for hers, and informing her repeatedly that he won't know what to do when she goes away. Other than a vase of flowers (used almost immediately as a prop) and a few other simple pieces of furniture, the room is extremely bare.

It becomes easy to focus on the obvious: the existence of the crumbling portrait of Clara. It's not a subtle message at all, nor is it a difficult one to fathom, as we see the Doctor sitting opposite the portrait looking more than a little like a grieving widower.

However, what we miss by focusing on the presence of the portrait is the **absence** of pretty much anything else. The furniture is typical plain bedroom furniture. No books, no other art, no mementos of any kind. It's an extremely barren inner sanctum for a 2,000-year-old time traveller with as much human interaction as he's had. One

---

[13] Moffat, '**Doctor Who** *Heaven Sent*: Blue Amendments', p11.

might expect a little photograph of his granddaughter, maybe a TARDIS blue diary on the nightstand[14]. But the most colourful thing in the room is a vase of flowers, and even those are relegated to clues in a puzzle.

Except that we are looking at the Doctor in this particular stage of his life. As we've said before, he shuns the contact of all but one person. His methods are notably more logical when a day needs saving, and he deliberately places distance between himself and just about anyone and anything else so he can manage that. It would be a cruel and almost certainly untrue leap to assume he's let go of every memory and loved one until now. But in his life as it stands, where he has almost completely come to terms with the fact that everyone leaves and everything ends, there is one person for whom he cannot reconcile that. He has pinned everything on her to the exclusion of everything else, even memories and reminiscences of family and companions past.

And now, confronted with this, the Doctor falls. For a very long time. And as he falls, we find him in another room that isn't technically built into the castle, but is still important to the story: the 'storm room'. However, the storm room gets a section all to itself, because while it is a very important part of the Doctor's grief and development, it's representative of an entirely separate facet of the Doctor's experience: that is, the Doctor as a persona rather than a

---

[14] His study in *The Pilot* (2017) and later stories is far more what one might imagine for this sort of room, and that room's choice of props and décor – from photos of Susan and River to a statuette of a raven – could fall comfortably into this same level of 'inner sanctum' analysis.

person. This bears a great deal of looking into separately, so for now we'll meet him on the opposite end of his trip out of the window: underwater in the castle moat.

The Plunge

Here we find the Doctor actually encountering the skulls – the same skull, really – for the first time. And here we are at what is arguably the lowest point, at least geographically, of the castle (until Room 12), seeing as we are now below sea level. Now, having sat opposite his deteriorating memories of Clara in the innermost parts of his hearts, he's sunk all the way down and is staring thousands of years' (so far) worth of death in the face. Again, it's very tempting to assign the death he's staring in the face to himself because the skulls, as we'll learn, are his. But remember that it took him no time at all to admit **that** fear. Just because he's convinced that's what he's dealing with doesn't mean that's what he's dealing with. The Doctor is as unreliable a narrator as they come[15], and he isn't about to start being reliable just because he's alone.

Note, too, that with the context of the entire episode comes the knowledge that this ever-growing pile of skulls is a symbol of his failure. The two – at least to him – go hand-in-hand. The death of a companion, especially of the companion he considered most like himself (to the point of 'showing her respect' in some very unpleasant ways[16]), counts to him as a failing. It's a reading that only becomes clear in retrospect, and one the Doctor will probably never

---

[15] 'Rule one: the Doctor lies' (River Song, *The Big Bang* (2010)).

[16] *Kill the Moon* (2014).

understand on sight, given how the time loop works.

What's interesting to note, though, is the placement of this moat. We know that the castle is, by necessity for foreshadowing, shaped like and functional as a dial, with the tower he arrives in serving as the centre. The moat he falls into is between the outer dial and the hub.

What in the world sort of castle has a moat on the inside? Moats are protection. They are a gulf between our home and things that could potentially harm us. And here, the Doctor's castle – the Doctor's inner sanctum – has a moat protecting its insides from its outsides. Not surprising, really, for a man who blatantly built a wall between himself and his one friend during his first episode, then spent the next 22 episodes trying to tear it down.

Now, we come to the part of the story where things become a little less clear in terms of the level of the castle the Doctor is on at any given time. It won't be hugely important, fortunately, as the majority of the rooms speak for themselves. When it is, it's fairly evident.

Inside and Outside

The Doctor makes an early pass through the kitchen that will be more important in a later chapter – where we have a look at what happened during his earlier runs through the castle. He then finds himself chased by the Veil into an atrium containing a garden and what might as well be a grave[17]. Here is where the Doctor begins to really latch back into his long game in the castle. He finds the paving stone that will eventually lead him to Room 12, left there for him by

---

[17] Moffat, *Heaven Sent*, p30.

'someone' who spent a great deal of time on it. This is also the first point at which he looks up at the stars and notices that something about the night sky is more than a little amiss.

In his book *Psychology and Alchemy* (1968), Jung examines the concept of the garden as a tame, orderly space – that is, in juxtaposition with a forest or wilderness, which would be more representative of one's subconscious[18]. Gardens are places where the wilds of nature are tamed, cared for, and put into order.

The Doctor's mind is a fairly wild place, the 12th Doctor's potentially more than most. We see this from his earliest moments, when his mind is so overflowing with knowledge that he has to scribble it across the entirety of a bedroom floor[19]. We see it throughout the majority of his episodes, where chalkboards litter the TARDIS in case an idea needs getting out – a necessity so alien to the Doctor that one of his former selves can't even understand it[20]. And we see it early in *The Witch's Familiar*, in Missy's '[c]onsider the Doctor' speech, as we are shown how all the elements of that larger-than-life mind can come together to make things happen in a matter of moments.

If the Doctor is a collection of personality traits that take turns coming to the forefront, this is yet another that has been especially notable with the 12th Doctor: where other regenerations' intelligence has been masked or tempered or otherwise downplayed, here his genius is an integral part of his portrayal, to the point that it affects his ability to interact with people of lesser

---

[18] Jung, Carl, *Psychology and Alchemy,* p186.
[19] *Deep Breath.*
[20] *Twice Upon a Time.*

intelligence even more than usual. So, to opt for the imagery of a garden, a place where we tame and trim back and control what would otherwise grow wild, is fitting for the Doctor, especially **this** Doctor, when the time comes for him to start working things out.

(As an aside, Jung also notes that gardens are an inherently feminine symbol[21]; fitting again, as recognition of the Doctor's lost taming influence, whom he keeps consulting in some form even in her absence – though whether or not it's actually **her** he's consulting is another issue entirely.)

Another narrow escape from the Veil, and now we step aside for a bit into an exploration of the Doctor's new day-to-day routine. He's learning the interior of his castle: its operation, the jumbled nature of its rooms, and how long it takes for the Veil to follow him from one end to the other. He's piecing it apart like the giant clockwork machine it is – a very Doctorish thing to do, until you layer the metaphorical nature of the castle over it.

The Doctor's uncertainty as to his ability to 'stay the course' is a mainstay of his persona, and one that will be explored more in its own chapter. But in the 12th Doctor, we see an incarnation that is not only willing to turn inward and analyse himself, but really quite desperate to. It's the not-so-secret story arc of the entirety of series 8, and even in series 9 he's not done picking things apart – and he won't finish until moments before he speaks his final words. Now, the Doctor doesn't stop at simply fearing his own nature or using his potential as a threat; he needs to explore, to understand, the way he

---

[21] Jung, *Psychology and Alchemy,* p186.

(the Doctor in general, the 12th Doctor in particular) is compelled to gain understanding of anything that is unfamiliar to him.

The Final Square

After this, we come back to the room where the Doctor started: the teleport room. Here, though, he notices things that were previously present but went ignored (by both the Doctor and the camera) during his opening monologue: the skull, and the simple note 'BIRD.' Now he is revisiting previous thoughts and experiences, but seeing them anew. Now that he's been to the garden (where his conscious mind can put things in order) and had time to deconstruct the castle by the numbers, he's re-evaluating.

Here, the Doctor's discoveries exist on two levels. On the first, he has discovered clues to complete his 4,5000,000,000-year run through the castle. On the second, he has discovered two things that very much define who he is and why he's here. The skull, we've discussed; the bird metaphor, we will discuss later, but simply having the new perspective will lead us into 'end game' for this particular run. Also with his new focus, he's found the way to the highest point in the castle.

Remember early on that we established – or, rather, Jung established – that the higher one is in one's 'house,' the closer one is to the conscious mind. Two things happen here of great importance, at the forefront of the Doctor's mind. First, most obviously, he notices the stars, giving him one of the final clues he needs to remember his trajectory through the castle. It doesn't quite hit home until he enters Room 12, but the information is present. The second, the confession he considered so personal that he saved it for last – his own fear – finally leads him to the last room, where everything becomes clear.

Room 12 is not mapped specifically in the castle. We know only that the Doctor has to go downstairs to enter it; but as he was at the very top of the castle, this is not entirely helpful. As mentioned before, it does give off a sense of being underground, almost cave-like in its structure, helped along by the far wall being constructed entirely of what is essentially super-hard diamond. This is potentially another callback to the primal room in Jung's dream, this time far closer to serving the same purpose.

Here, as the Doctor tells 'Clara' in his storm room, is where he 'always' remembers. He has descended immediately from his conscious mind to his subconscious, and while the decision-making takes place in its own separate venue, Room 12 is where the Doctor reverts to the most primal of problem-solving methods: punching things. (Yes, there is a carefully planned course of action behind this, but at the end of the day it's his fists that do the talking.)

As to the diamond wall – technically Azbantium, but aesthetically and symbolically and visually it's a diamond wall – in his seminar 'Children's Dreams,' Jung addresses a participant who asks about the nature of diamond and diamond-like substances from a symbolic standpoint. Jung points out the origin of diamonds: in essence, super-hardened earth, a base matter that has been compressed over time to create something beautiful and transparent. In that way, if we take 'earth' to refer to the human (or humanoid) body, the diamond created from it is its ultimate potential, its form when granted time and attaining clarity[22].

So now, we've reached by rights what should be the end of the Doctor's journey of introspection: the deepest part of his subconscious, placing him opposite a fairly grand symbol of his own potential, which will open and release him from this constant cycle of introspection provided he takes that final step in confession and self-discovery. That is, essentially, where this is all meant to end. The fact that he chooses otherwise is the subject of its own chapter, as well as the reason why we've still got a way to go in this one.

Until the Doctor finally gets through the Azbantium wall **his** way, the end point of his journey through the castle is not Room 12, but the beginning and midpoint: the teleport chamber. He'll do the same thing again and again (presumably with an occasional different route, always a bit longer punching through the wall) for four and a half billion years, but he will always find himself back at his starting point: surrounded by signs of death and the remnants of his own failure, having ultimately unlocked all the necessary rooms but landing right back where he started.

The End?

Were this any other story about any other character, we might still be tempted to call the Doctor's exploration of the castle complete, satisfactory, or successful. The rooms serve their purpose, he finds what he needs to, and along the way (as we will see) he does make some discoveries about himself. And that really is what this is all

---

[22] Jung, Carl, *Children's Dreams: Notes from the Seminar Given in 1936-1940*, pp 221-223.

about, right?

Well, no.

On the most basic of levels, we've explored the Doctor's bespoke torture chamber, and thus to a degree his psyche: places of high thought and discovery, a barren inner sanctum that is more notable for what it lacks than what it contains, a place where his overflowing intellect can be tamed and put to good use, many points (both high and low) that serve as reminders of what he's lost and what else he stands to lose. On its own, as a stable, unchanging building, it already serves its purpose.

But this is the Doctor. His personality changes every handful of years, a trait that significantly alters things both within the plot and on a metatextual basis. And this is the 12th Doctor: analytical, dangerously curious, vulnerable, and facing all the things that a person can have done to them when they are that combination of traits. He is also battling extreme grief, which, as anyone who's been through it will tell you, can turn your insides into a shifting mess on its own.

So, while the venues within the Confession Dial may beg a close examination of their function, that function becomes irrelevant without change and movement. This means not only the ever-present gears that have become a trademark of the 12th Doctor's era, but also the Veil – our 'monster of the week,' as it were. And a mind as ancient and vast as the Doctor's takes a lot of exploration and unlocking.

With that in mind, and knowing what each room represents and what it's for, we move on to how it functions, how the Doctor is

supposed to operate it, and what exactly – other than being overall quite creepy – the Veil is for.

CHAPTER 2: THE FINAL NIGHTMARE

The 'villains' throughout the 12th Doctor's time with Clara – be they genuine villains or simply antagonists the Doctor assigns himself – have largely been representative of the Doctor himself, or of some aspect of himself that he resents or fears. Series 8 brings us a constantly reinvented faux human who can't remember where he got his face, a warrior of dubious morality who insists he is good, an unreal folk hero, and an ever-regenerating soldier whose war has long since passed... to name but a few[23]. One episode even pits the Doctor's own paranoia against him[24] in what is potentially the show's first and finest depiction of night blogging[25].

The intensity of the parallels tapers somewhat in series 9, once the 'Am I a good man?' question has been as resolved as it can ever be for the Doctor, but parallels still exist. At this point, though, they are at best examples of results of his intervention first and foremost, and mirrors second. Davros, Ashildr, Bonnie the Zygon, and eventually Clara herself all became what they are as results of the Doctor's well-meaning meddling, for better or for worse. And, in the process, they all became a bit Doctory in their own way.

The Veil, though, harkens back more to the theme of *Listen* (2014), where the antagonist (or at least our antagonist stand-in) is less an

---

[23] *Deep Breath*, *Into the Dalek*, *Robot of Sherwood*, and *Mummy on the Orient Express* (all 2014).
[24] *Listen* (2014).
[25] A Tumblr phenomenon where bloggers awake during the wee hours begin posting surreal, introspective observations – everything from 'The brain named itself' to 'I wish I cried macaroni because then I'd have free macaroni all the time.'

aspect of the Doctor and more an internal fear. On the surface, in the Veil's case, that fear seems fairly obvious: she's constructed from what we can assume to be the Doctor's first view of a corpse, and she's attended by buzzing flies, so it's a fear of death.

That said, we established a chapter ago that the Doctor's fear of his **own** death is probably not what's on the table right now. A Time Lord's engagement with the concept of mortality is a tricky one, and the Doctor's was already explored more than sufficiently in 2013. Rather, as stated, we're dealing with an examination of grief – grief and guilt, because for someone like the Doctor, the two tend to go hand in hand. Companions have died, disappeared, or suffered death of personality on multiple occasions either due to their direct actions or because those companions became as brave and driven as the Doctor without regenerative abilities to bring them back.

Another Shadow

We can't dive too far into a discussion of the Veil without touching on her immediate function from a psychological and storytelling standpoint. Already addressed as a 'shadow' as soon as the Doctor enters the Confession Dial, the Veil can, in her own way, be seen to fulfil that role to at least some degree.

The concept of the Shadow, according to Jung, is our literal 'dark side.' This could be the parts of ourselves that we personally dislike or do not identify with, or aspects of ourselves that are truly and objectively bad from a moral or social standpoint. In the world of fiction, a hero can either defeat their Shadow or come to terms with it. However, in real-world psychology, we are encouraged to make peace with our Shadow, and see it as a part of us rather than something to be shunned or feared.

The Doctor has already had multiple Shadow selves manifest in the television series. The Valeyard of *The Trial of a Time Lord* (1986), a personification of the Doctor 'somewhere between [his] twelfth and final incarnations,' was a very literal embodiment of the evil within the Doctor. The 11th Doctor's run also presented us with the Dream Lord[26] and 'Mr Clever'[27], two more iterations of the Doctor's darker and crueller side.

However, with the Veil, we do not see the Doctor's fear and hatred of his own darker tendencies manifest. Rather, we see a creeping, rotting terror whose job is to bring those fears and darker tendencies to the surface in his own words. Thus, she isn't technically his Shadow herself – but she does give it form. Her approach means that he will soon need to dig into his own thoughts and emerge with a confession. She herself is not the darkness – merely the harbinger thereof. And this function is what sets the entire castle into motion.

The Clockwork

Despite the Doctor's longevity (which it's safe at this point to code as immortality), death does follow him, as his friends and enemies are more than happy to point out on a regular basis. This is often taken in the 'Oncoming Storm' sense, but the amount of death, near death, or might-as-well-be-death that befalls the very breakable humans he cares about is just as justifiable a reading for this criticism, if not more. The audio tie-in play *Scherzo* (2003) (a two-hander written by Rob Shearman, the scriptwriter of *Dalek* (2005)), suggests that the Time Lords view the Doctor's companions as 'mementi mori':

---

[26] *Amy's Choice* (2010).
[27] *Nightmare in Silver* (2013).

reminders of mortality to counteract his own seeming invulnerability. While the television series never goes so far as to assume that that's a purpose for which the companions are kept on the TARDIS, series 9 does reflect the Doctor's awareness of this even before *Heaven Sent*. Clara's presence is a constant reminder of something that could – and will – eventually disappear from his world, even with her assurances that she isn't going anywhere[28].

Time Lord logic doesn't have the best of track records, but even if the outcome wasn't intentional, the fact remains: human companions are breakable, killable, and have a finite life span even if they do survive their time with the Doctor. There will come a time, no matter how well his latest stray turns out, when he will never ever see them again[29]. So, the Doctor may not keep companions on board for that specific purpose, but the purpose is served nonetheless.

How appropriate, then, for the Doctor's bespoke torture chamber to be operated primarily by his engagement with the manifestation of his concept of grief (and thus guilt). Because the Veil – or, more specifically, how the Doctor interacts with her – is the key to operating the Confession Dial, as well as our clue early on that this is a confessional.

---

[28] *The Woman Who Lived* (2015).

[29] This applies even in the modern era of guest appearances and throwbacks, due largely – sadly – to the fact that the human lifespan is not a fictional conceit. While actors' deaths are not always written into the plot of the series, moments such as the attention Nicholas Courtney's loss was given in *The Wedding of River Song* (2011) drive the point home on multiple layers.

All the clues we need for how the Dial works are shown, not told, many of them in the cinematography. We figure it out along with the Doctor. The Veil plods along ceaselessly toward him until she has him cornered, at which point he must confess a truth of some degree. Once he's done this, the Dial turns, allowing access to more parts of the castle.

When we look at the castle, as we did in the previous chapter, as a reflection of the Doctor's psyche, and certain rooms as difficult-to-access parts of it, the operation of the Dial is straightforward. Self-examination, confession in the face of grief and guilt, and some degree of acceptance will open the path to realisation and, one is led to believe, an eventual escape. Small truths do a little; big truths do a lot. Theoretically, the ultimate truth – or, at least, the ultimate truth the Time Lords want (which is not that big a deal in this particular narrative) – will open the diamond wall that will take the Doctor home.

And refusing to answer means... death? So it would seem, at least within the confines of this castle. More accurately, it means simply not being allowed to leave – perhaps a reference, knowing or otherwise, to the Buddhist concept of samsara. The Doctor's wandering, literally cyclical as he is 'reborn' into the Dial for millennia tracing the same path, will come to an end only through the attainment of a personal enlightenment.

In this way, we can see both the narrative use of the Confession Dial and, within the story structure, its almost purgatorial nature. Were it not for the Dial's setup in *The Magician's Apprentice*, it would exist solely as a Character Development Machine. Which it is, of course, but the MO fits the Time Lord aesthetic well. Plus, as with the best of Time Lord technology[30], it can be manipulated and used for other purposes – as it has been here.

It's also easily manipulated for metatextual purposes – just as the Confession Dial is, at its core, a Character Development Machine, this is a Character Development Episode by design. And the function of the castle is just as important as the layout. The way the gears turn is as important as the gears themselves.

Freddy's Dead

At the Intervention 7 convention in Rockville, Maryland, director Rachel Talalay presented a miniature masterclass on *Heaven Sent*[31], in which she explained her inspiration and design for the Veil. Her instructions were to make it, and to make everything, both beautiful and terrifying. No small feat, as much of horror now relies on the grotesque.

Her inspiration came from a variety of places. She cited *Citizen Kane* and German expressionism for much of the episode's aesthetic. But when it came to the Veil herself, Talalay went back to another of her directorial projects: *Freddy's Dead: The Final Nightmare* (1991).

The sixth film in the **A Nightmare on Elm Street** series, *Freddy's Dead* is anything but subtle or beautiful. It is the sort of entry you would expect in a modern American horror series: gore aplenty, ludicrous body horror, and deliberate cheesiness. Comparing the Veil to Freddy is not something one would immediately think to do, even after watching the two side by side and knowing they're both works by

---

[30] As 'best' as the technology of a race that creates pocket torture confessionals and sentient reset buttons can be considered.
[31] For which I served as moderator.

Talalay. However, it's the process – not the result – that is comparable.

Freddy's Dead is, in its own way, a character development story, as we see Freddy Krueger's daughter coming to terms with her lineage and throwing off her father's control over her (both literally and subconsciously). 'Subtlety' is not a word that shows up in Freddy's playbook – in his hauntings the grotesque and the slapstick compete, with the gore only marginally warding off the laughter of his ludicrous punishments. At least, that's true of most of his victims. His hold over his daughter is much more creeping, much more sinister, than for his run-of-the-mill victims. And that's where we begin to see some *Heaven Sent* parallels.

In *Freddy's Dead*, much of the horror is blatant, visual, even nauseating. But what you **don't** see is often more terrifying than what you **do** see. The true points of terror come when Freddy, as well as we know him at this point, isn't actually in shot… or when he's only **barely** in shot.

One of Talalay's tricks with the Veil is to place her in the foreground, showing just a hand, or just a bit of her back. That closeness to the subject of terror, while still seeing relatively little of her, hammers home the point: she is inescapable. She is tireless. She is always there. To paraphrase the Doctor in series 10's *Smile* (2017), things that don't run after you are all the more frightening because it means they don't **have** to run.

That supplies us with the 'terrifying,' but not with the 'beautiful.' There is very little beautiful about something that walks tirelessly and wants you dead. The castle, with individual lights outside each window to cast atmospheric beams, is beautiful and terrifying. But the Veil is a literal corpse.

Also during the Intervention masterclass, Talalay discussed early designs for the Veil, which started as much more grotesque than what we end up seeing in the actual episode. These early designs called for something far more twisted and visually upsetting. The designs were toned down until we were left with a veiled, seemingly faceless creature, with only two genuinely grotesque points: the flies that signal her presence, and the monstrous, corpselike hands that reach out for her victim when she draws near.

It doesn't take much effort to imagine that the Doctor would be haunted by a spectre of death that has an aspect of beauty to it. He's lived long and he's curious. Even a younger Doctor refers to death as 'someplace [he's] never been' and seems rather childishly intrigued by it[32]. But with the 12th Doctor especially – a Doctor influenced both by his typical need-to-know-ness that's nearly gotten him killed[33] and his actor's love of the macabre – a beautiful, almost romantic Grim Reaper image seems somehow fitting.

It becomes apparent, as soon as the Doctor makes his first confession to the Veil, that the Veil and the castle are intrinsically linked. She is a mechanism of it (as is revealed rather blatantly during her final moments when she collapses into a pile of gears) – as much a fixture within the castle as the rotating rooms and the abzantium wall. One

---

[32] *Doctor Who* (1996), in which the sentimental old TARDIS resurrects Grace and Chang. Grace tells the Doctor that it's 'nothing to be scared of' with much the same tone as someone describing a flu shot.

[33] *Listen* yet again.

might go so far as to say she's the castle's 'interface' with the Doctor: the bit that makes the whole thing work.

Breaking the Game

So now, we must look back at the purpose of the Confession Dial and how it works. According to the inscription on the wall, and as demonstrated by the Doctor's ultimately fatal repeated encounters with her, one would rightly assume that the Veil's purpose is to kill him. But that makes no sense, for a pair of reasons.

Firstly, the Doctor has been placed here by the Time Lords, who want information out of him. A dead Doctor does them no good. If we come to the point where we've killed our informant, the information dies with them and we're even more at a loss than when we started.

But secondly – and potentially more tellingly – this is the Doctor's Confession Dial. It wasn't created by the Time Lords specifically to get information about the Hybrid out of him. It already existed, as Missy showed us in *The Magician's Apprentice*. It's even conceivable that it was already situated to beat the Doctor up for a single piece of information. In which case, what good is an end-of-life confessional that kills you? You're already going to die; it would be redundant.

Thus, we can assume that the death, replication, and repetition are **a deliberately manufactured element of the Confession Dial.** The Doctor didn't 'break the game' – he was always meant to get caught in a time loop. Else why would it be a possibility? Why would the occasion for his 'death' and 'rebooting' be available in the first place?

Remember that the Confession Dial is a piece of technology – Time Lord technology, but technology nonetheless. And technology cannot do anything more than it was programmed to do. The Doctor is brilliant, but short of genuine reprogramming, isn't capable of making a machine behave in a way it was created not to – especially when he is **within** the machine, at its mercy[34].

Think of modern video games, which allow 'freedom' for the player. The player isn't actually given freedom to defy what the game wants, because games don't work like that. Anything a player can do within a game has already been accounted for, dictated, and coded. If you're allowed to drive a car off-road, kill a quest-giver, or choose to spare a villain, it's because the programmer decided in advance that you could. You are no freer of invisible walls than you've ever been.

This is a difficult point to present with any sort of credibility, as we live in an era of mods and speed runs. But video games as they are now cannot have their structures altered **on the fly** when we are in the position of the character. On the back end, modifying the code, we can enable characters to fly or clip through walls. But when we are in direct engagement, we are subject to the whims of the programmer. If the programmer has made a game in which our only goal is to get from point A to point B and they have not accounted for any other points, those points will not exist in the game. Elements only exist if they are to be interacted with.

---

[34] The only potential example of this might be his stunt in the following series' *Extremis* (2017). We could potentially come up with workarounds for this discrepancy, but the easiest answer is a metatextual one: Moffat was playing a similar scenario for a different endgame. The Confession Dial and the virtual universe of *Extremis* serve two different story purposes, the former of which we will continue to explore here.

For example, 'pacifist runs' of games – playthroughs in which a gamer manages to complete a game (usually an extremely violent one) without personally killing a single character – would not be possible if the programmers did not allow it. If it was inherently necessary to the game's play style or plot to have the main character shed blood, it would be easy to code in a requirement to do so. This has not changed the ending or purpose of the game; it has only been an exercise in playing within the game's set code.

Similarly, it is highly unlikely that the Doctor – even the brilliant engineer 12th with all his intelligence – was actually subverting the mechanics of the Confession Dial by burning himself to make copies. The opportunities and resources were there; and in programming terms – which apply if we consider the Dial's interior to be virtual in nature – that means it is a path that the makers expected the Doctor to take.

Also take into account that he eventually remembers the entire cycle. There's been some argument among the fan base as to whether the Doctor's 4,500,000,000 years in the Dial count as an addition to his already vast lifespan – thus introducing the question of whether the constantly rebooted copy of the Doctor is the 'real' Doctor any more.

However, the Doctor always remembers the time loop eventually – which wouldn't seem possible in a fresh copy. Also, when Clara asks how long the Doctor was in the Confession Dial, Ohila responds: 'We think four and a half billion years.'[35] The vague uncertainty betrays that time within the Confession Dial does not correlate to time

---

[35] *Hell Bent.*

outside it, and for all anyone knows it could have been a few seconds[36]. So rather than the Doctor actually burning himself over and over to make copies, it is more likely that the 'death' and 'rebirth' elements were part of a very realistic, very unpleasant, simulation.

Finally, there are 'resets' to be taken into account. Which rooms reset, as well as when and how, seems very convenient. Theoretically, the entire castle goes back to the beginning whenever the Doctor burns himself up and resets. But think of what remains the same from one run to another: Clara's portrait, slowly decaying; the extra pair of clothes drying by the fire, left by his 'previous self'; suspicious clues left for himself here and there (which will be the subject of the next chapter); and, worst of all, an ever-growing pile of skulls. The things that don't reset seem almost tailor-made to serve as a trail of breadcrumbs: enough to serve up a mystery befitting the Doctor's insatiable curiosity, but discouraging enough when they're all pieced together to drive him to the point of surrender.

With those facts in place, it becomes apparent that the Veil's function in the Doctor's Dial was not just confessor, but also executioner: the function by which the time loop would swing into action. The loops – to a point – were part of the plan. The Doctor didn't hack the system (at least, not at first) – he played within it exactly as he was intended to. Granted, this would eventually fall apart, but for the time being, all we need to know is that he was

---

[36] One could argue 'Time Lord technology' as usual, which probably comes into play in Confession Dials in general. Still, that doesn't necessarily serve as an argument against the dial being of a more 'virtual' nature.

almost certainly meant to suffer and acknowledge this time loop.

So, with all this in mind, we can begin to lay out what the intended mechanics (in a very literal sense, given the castle's clockwork motif) of the Confession Dial are:

1. The Doctor enters.
2. The Doctor discovers the Veil.
3. The Doctor figures out that the Veil can only be stopped if he confesses a dark secret.
4. The Doctor – because of who he is – embarks on an investigation of the castle and its purpose.
5. During this run, the Doctor discovers just enough clues to lay a groundwork for the answer.
6. The Doctor discovers the answer.
7. **The Doctor despairs**.
8. Eventually, when despair has truly taken hold, the Doctor tells what he knows of the Hybrid so that he can be freed of the time loop.

Not only is the time loop an essential part of the experience, but so is **despair**. This, more than anything else, would finally give us our answer when it comes to why certain rooms reset and others didn't. Fan theories have operated under the assumption that there's some sort of mechanic that was ignored, and that things like the Doctor's dry clothes, his ever-growing pile of skulls, and the scrawling of 'BIRD' stumbled conveniently through a plot hole.

But how could that be the case in his bespoke murder castle? How could there be mechanical flaws in a castle that is fitted specifically to the nature of the 12th Doctor, of all incarnations – one who could, in a heartbeat, go and crack those flaws wide open and bring the whole situation crashing down?

The rooms that don't reset are neither arbitrary nor wasted. Each one is a puzzle piece that will lead him to his end point:

The dust lays the groundwork. It gives him something to think back to – the painful knowledge that he had the answer as soon as he stepped out of the transporter. The harsh symbolism of stepping in and over and through his own remains time after time after time. There's a reason this room is the beginning, middle, and end point of each cycle: it allows him to revisit the scene of his 'defeat' multiple times, with more and growing context each time.

The portrait of Clara – which (according to Steven Moffat) the 'soppy' Doctor painted himself – continues to crumble. In a true hard reset, the portrait would cease to exist entirely. Here, the Doctor has helped the castle along, actually. The portrait, slowly decaying, is a one-two punch: not only a reminder of time passing for him, but also of the fragility of human life – of Clara's life.

The ever-growing pile of skulls is the terrifying tell. Moffat claims that anything outside the castle won't be reset, which would presumably include the moat[37]. However, even without this explanation, the growing mountain of Doctor skulls still serves its purpose within the function of the castle increasing his despair[38].

---

[37] Fullerton, Huw, 'Steven Moffat Has Filled in the "Plot Holes" from **Doctor Who**: *Heaven Sent*'.

[38] Clever mathematician fans have worked out that, by the time the Doctor finally busts through the wall, the pile of skulls will potentially be piling along the edge of the moat and up the castle walls. That should do the trick.

The Doctor's dry clothes supply that first moment of suspicion. For a Doctor as clever as the 12th, this is probably when the first puzzle piece snapped in – when he entertained the idea but refused to believe it. They're also necessary, of course – though according to an interview with Moffat on the *Radio Times* website, there was a 'generic' set of clothes waiting on his first go round[39].

The deliberate clues are the Doctor unwittingly working against himself. Anyone constructing a Confession Dial would know how the Doctor works. So of course it behoves the Dial to let him pass his clues to himself. How else could he understand how hopeless his situation is?

And **the stars themselves** begin to hammer things home. This is the really telling bit: the moment when he can attach a **specific amount of time** to his battle. The moment he can think, 'I've been at this a thousand / a million / a billion years and I'm still stuck here.' Appropriately, this realisation is poised (as we discussed in the first chapter) at the highest point of the castle: the superconscious, where he is most aware.

It is also fair to assume that **his own death** is just as much a function of the Dial as anything else. Because it is here that he has put together everything for himself. This is where the true despair, and the full weight of what he is attempting to do, begins to set in. This is the point where he sees (and feels) the pointlessness of his journey. He will die, crawling through the remains of all his previous failures. And reconstruct himself. And be reduced to dust, just to

---

[39] Talalay, however, maintained in her Intervention 7 Q&A that the Doctor completed the first round naked.

repeat the whole thing over and over again. And at some point, he'll give up.

Considering that even Ohila was shocked at the length of his time in the Confession Dial, we can assume that was the plan. Because the **Azbantium wall** is the final element: one more thing that doesn't reset. Understandably, the slowly-whittled dent in that wall is essential to making sure the Doctor's despair continues to grow. But if the point is to make him eventually give in, then why was it possible for him to escape?

This is where things get a little hairy. Because it's essential for him to see how slow his own progress is. Perhaps it's a case like a video game boss with 9,999,999 hit points that you're meant to lose to, but remains beatable simply because no one believes any player has that patience. Or maybe some unknown 'someone' thought that if the Doctor really did chip away for that long, they wouldn't bother trying to stop him.

Either way, the Doctor is the Doctor, and the 12th Doctor even more so. Whether he knew it at the time or not, he helped himself. And he left his mark on the castle over the course of billions of years, altering it in such a way that not only would it eventually lead him to his end point, but it would also begin to reflect more and more of him and his journey through it.

CHAPTER 3: THE NET TIGHTENS

Of course, the Confession Dial does not stay the same for terribly long. We don't see the Doctor's first run through it – rather, we first witness one a few thousand years in: far enough that he's had some effect and left himself some clues, but not far enough that he can feel at all assured that he's getting out any time soon. In other words, far enough that he (and we) can despair, but not far enough that he (or we) can hope.

It is, of course, the way of the Doctor. Despite the Doctor's constant talk of 'fixed points,' with everything from Jack Harkness[40] to moon dragons[41], he can't claim that he's ever left a site untouched.

Making a Path

What's especially important about the non-resetting clues is that they occur throughout the castle. They aren't back-loaded, as they would be if the Doctor always figured out what was going on at the same pace. In his *Radio Times* interview, Moffat explains this:

> 'The first time round the castle, the Doctor is there for many years because there is no clue leading him to Room 12. He's ancient by the time he understands that Room 12 is important. [...] After a few thousand years of this, he realises he's going too slowly. He needs to get the next version of himself into Room 12 faster.'

So by the time **we** see the Doctor in the Confession Dial, he has already laid himself out a path. And this happens over runs that take

---

[40] *Utopia* (2007).
[41] *Kill the Moon.*

centuries, even millennia. And with 'our' run being 7,000 years in, with skulls and dust piled high, that means he managed to cut each run down to a tiny fraction of what it once was.

This also means that, during his first runs, he found ways to continue to evade the Veil. We see him timing how long it takes him, versus her, to get from one side of the castle to the other. And for a time, we see his new life living under these conditions. Going by what Moffat said, he lived this life for years, even centuries, as he worked out what to do. That said, the Doctor playing a centuries-long game isn't all that strange in the Moffat era[42]; this is potentially why a span of time as great as 4.5 billion years was needed for effect, since the Doctor waiting around a thousand or so years for something is becoming more and more commonplace.

Changes

Let us look, then, at what the Doctor believed to be essential clues to lead himself forward. After all, he would know what he needs, and he was (according to Moffat) attempting to counteract what he believed to be an indiscriminate total reset of the castle. We can make assumptions, as with the last chapter, that the function of the castle causes his fear of those resets to be pointless, but the Doctor does not have that information. He is working to the best of his knowledge, and the best of his knowledge states that his footprint will always be erased – therefore, he must leave as many clues as he can in as many places as he can, and hope that at least one will survive.

---

[42] *The Time of the Doctor* and *The Pandorica Opens* (2010) to name just two.

We start with one that is, to be fair, an intention of Moffat's rather than something that was actually shown as occurring in the story. In his breakdown of the episode, Moffat says that the Doctor's portrait of Clara had 'I AM IN 12' written on the back[43], as well. We never discover this, he goes on to say, because the Doctor could not bring himself to turn Clara's face to the wall.

This is a very important point beyond the obvious. In many cultures, especially old Orthodox Christianity, it is traditional to turn mirrors **and portraits of the deceased** toward the wall for a span of time following their death. This is to ensure that the spirit cannot re-enter its old home in the week or so following their death[44]. The custom is, of course, not limited to Middle Eastern Christianity, and will show up in entertainment on occasion, usually to denote heavy superstition.

The Doctor's bedroom in the castle, as we've already noted, is his 'inner sanctum'. And in this place, he not only creates an image of Clara, but wilfully refuses to prevent her 'haunting' him. Perhaps it's only a small note that never made it into the script and ultimately makes no great difference to the narrative. But how much sooner could he have stepped through his grief and found the doorway to 'Home' had he simply chosen to not let her haunt his thoughts?

This, though, is simply an aside by the writer – important for extra context, but not necessarily something we can dwell on when talking about the televised work. We do see the changes the Doctor began to make when he understood how the castle worked, and how he

---

[43] Fullerton, Huw, 'Steven Moffat has filled in the "plot holes"'.
[44] My family brought this tradition with them from Lebanon.

began to bring himself around to a faster and faster solution.

That main change is a bit of a puzzling one: removing a piece of flooring from the kitchen, inscribing 'I AM IN 12' on it, and then burying it in the courtyard garden with a shovel nearby. According to Moffat[45], the paving slab (and the portrait, if you like) were not the only places this clue was written. Apparently it was 'all over the castle,' with the paving slab being the one regularly found[46].

But there's nothing immediately logical about the method: removing a paving slab from a random room, drawing arrows around it, and that's it? Few viewers caught on the first (or second or third) go that the paving slab missing from the kitchen was the same as the great stone slab buried in the garden. One could be generous and say it was meant to be open-ended and unintuitive in order to escape the castle's reset, but a potentially more even-handed theory is that it was an instance of a writer being so used to an idea that they forgot to clarify it in the finished product.

Nonetheless, even if it were perfectly clear that the paving slab was also the stone in the garden... **why?** The idea smacks more of a room escape game than something that would come from the mind of the extremely linear 12th Doctor. 'Find something that looks like this. By the way, it's completely buried, so don't bother actually looking for anything this shape.'

---

[45] Fullerton, Huw, 'Steven Moffat has filled in the "plot holes"'.
[46] This doesn't necessarily mean it's the only one that doesn't get reset. We have no way of knowing that. And again, we are only seeing one run – it's fair to assume that he found different clues on different runs that we don't see, and perhaps missed the paving stone entirely in others.

A very simplistic reason goes back to the Doctor starting to understand what he believes to be the 'reset' function of the castle. He needs to scrawl himself a message. He apparently has enough knowledge on other runs to see that rooms reset themselves – perhaps in earlier runs he revisits rooms he saw a few days before and gathers this. It seems like a move of desperation... and perhaps it was. Prying up a paving slab and burying it outside with the only clues being a gap (that could get reset) and chalk arrows (that could also get reset) seems almost like a last resort – a throwing-in of the towel. As mentioned before, it could be little more than an idea whose explanation didn't survive edits. As interesting as the scene is visually, we're missing enough information to trace back the thought process in any sort of meaningful way.

Then again, there could be many, many things like this throughout the castle that are never seen. If, as Moffat says, the Doctor left these clues 'everywhere,' we can most probably take that literally. The engineer-minded 12th Doctor, unable to predict which rooms reset and why, would most likely spend a good portion of his longer runs scrawling the message in every room possible. Potentially, the paving slab remained simply because it was so non-linear. Or because it was so difficult to get to. He may in fact have lost all his clues save for this one that he (literally) had to dig for, as part of the castle's function to give him just enough to drive him to hope, then desperation.

The Shepherd Boy

Of course, the biggest clue – the lynchpin of the entire exercise – is the story of the shepherd boy and the king. The Doctor's truncated version, in which the boy explains to a king how to count the seconds in eternity, tells only a sliver of the (admittedly short) tale.

'The Shepherd Boy' is one of the shorter stories in the Brothers Grimm's repertoire – around a page or less in a bound edition. The shepherd boy of the story is actually famous in his kingdom for answering questions wisely. A king disbelieves that a mere shepherd boy could be so wise and goes to the boy with three questions. If the boy can answer all three satisfactorily, the king will take him away to the palace and treat him as a son.

The story of the bird and the diamond mountain is the shepherd's answer to the last of the three questions. However, the previous two are similarly broad: the king asks how many drops of water there are in an ocean and how many stars there are in the sky. In response to the first, the boy requests that the king dam up every ocean, river, and stream in the world, and give the boy time to count each drop himself. And to the second, the boy covers a sheet of paper with dots of ink until it is nearly sold black, then asks the king to count them – which, of course, he cannot.

Of course, there is a direct parallel between the bird chipping away at a diamond mountain and the Doctor chipping away at the Azbantium wall. One single word, in context, is enough to give him as much of a clue as he needs for his millennia-long scheme.

Interestingly, though, the comparison doesn't end there. The Doctor's time in the castle seems to follow the framing device of this fairy tale in a number of ways. First, and most obviously, the time devoted to tedious and pointless-seeming tasks – the in-built despair mentioned in the previous chapter. Just as the shepherd boy invites the king to count a page of ink dots or dam up all the water in the world so it can be counted drop by drop, the Doctor finds himself picking away day after day at a problem that eventually takes billions of years to solve... with a backslide each time he finally gets back to the Azbantium wall. The whole castle is, in essence, on par with one of the king's requests.

But besides this, we find the three themes of the questions – the ocean, the stars, and the mountain – matching the three primary 'beats' of the Doctor's time in the castle. The moat, filled with thousands of carbon copies of his own skull. The stars, inching along through the sky as he counts off the years on each run. And, of course, the wall, which he picks away at on each run. And the Gallifreyan boy at the end, described as 'the equivalent of a shepherd's boy' in the writer's room script available online[47], brings the whole thing around once more at the end – just in case we've forgotten.

In this way, one could potentially see the Doctor as both the king and the shepherd boy in this equation: both the disbelieving, powerful figure in search of answers, and the childish vagabond with unexpected wisdom. He is his own self-contained version of this story, answering his own questions and demonstrating the vastness and futility of the eternity he potentially faces; and yet, he eventually conquers each of these impossible psychological exercises and finds his way home[48].

However, the Doctor most definitely does not see himself as either of these. It's true that 'BIRD' is, from a technical level, the easiest thing you could give to him when he faces down a diamond wall in an eternal purgatory. He'd understand that. He knows the story. But

---

[47] Moffat, '*Heaven Sent*: Blue Amendments', p92.
[48] Which is a far less happy ending than the shepherd boy got.

52

in giving himself this clue, he is casting himself as the bird, which is practically little more than a prop in the fairy tale. The bird has one job: fly out, whittle on the mountain, leave.

With this in mind, think back to our first impression of this Doctor: a man who may or may not have killed a sentient robot, leaving us only a fourth-wall-breaking glare to work from[49]. A man who, as mentioned, utilised a good-as-dead stranger to save the ones who had a chance of living[50]. A man whose entire first story arc was built upon his oldest frenemy gathering up the people who died (albeit indirectly) at his hands in the midst of his plans to save the universe.

Granted, such characters have always been a feature of the Doctor's life. The heavy focus on the humanity of his collateral damage is a 21st century move, but they've always been there. And in the recent life of the show, this has been handled with at least some degree of delicacy by giving the Doctor a chance to apologise tearfully or throw them a mournful Lonely God look showing that he knows this isn't good.

But the 12th Doctor, the engineer, only wants to get the job done. Good-as-dead people, those who have no chance of being saved, become tools – not because he devalues life, but (ironically) because he values it so much that he's able to make the tough, 'cold' calls[51]. And in the world of the Confession Dial, **he** is now the collateral damage.

---

[49] *Deep Breath*.
[50] *Into the Dalek*.
[51] His monologue to the Half-Faced Man in *Deep Breath*, in the midst of us questioning whether this new Doctor is safe or reliable, gives us some hope to that effect.

53

The greatest alteration the Doctor brought to the Dial is, funnily enough, himself. His willingness to turn himself into the disposable troops, to make himself a tool of his own plan, is something that even the Doctor himself may never have accounted for. He uses the Dial's mechanic of despair against itself. Rather than letting the repetition destroy him, he – **now** – manages to game the system. The few clues he leaves behind for himself don't reset because it is necessary he see them for the Dial to serve its purpose. But to transform himself into the very disposable helpers he's criticised for having in the first place is something that few, if any, counted on.

The question now is, was the Doctor acting 'in the name of the Doctor'? Or had the Doctor left the room at this point? To answer this question, we must understand who – and what – the Doctor is.

CHAPTER 4: DOCTOR WHO?

When we did our initial run-through of the rooms featured in the episode, there was one that was conspicuously left out: the storm room. There are a few reasons for this. For one thing, it's not technically part of the castle; for another, Jung doesn't talk much about imaginary TARDIS control rooms in his various theories.

But, most importantly, this room ties into something far greater and more important in the overall scheme of the story: the Doctor as the Doctor.

In *Face the Raven*, when Ashildr informs the Doctor that he'd never harm her out of revenge, he responds: 'The Doctor is no longer here! You are stuck with me.' This isn't the first time in Steven Moffat's tenure that the concept of the Doctor as **persona** rather than **person** has come up. The entirety of the 50th anniversary special hinged on this concept[52].

The question of who the Doctor really is, is one that fans both want and don't want answered more than anything. The series regularly plays with that dichotomy, as with the 2013 episode *The Name of the Doctor*. The title was relevant both to others' desire to learn the Doctor's name and to the invocation of the Doctor's personal moral code. However, the title on its own also lends suspense: will we learn the Doctor's name tonight? Do we **want** to know it?

Late in the 20th century series' run Andrew Cartmel, Marc Platt, and Ben Aaronovitch worked together on what fans (and DWM) ended

---

[52] *The Day of the Doctor* (2013). Moffat's 2018 novelisation of the anniversary story expands on this theme at length.

up dubbing the 'Cartmel Masterplan.' The idea was to create a genuine larger-than-life history for the Doctor, which would be unspooled slowly through the seasons that ended up not following[53]. Serials such as *Remembrance of the Daleks*, *Silver Nemesis* (both 1988) and *Battlefield* (1989) began to weave these threads in by giving the Doctor powers beyond even what a Time Lord can generally exhibit, but the BBC's decision not to renew the series left most of those actions in the lurch, though they were explored in Virgin Publishing's **New Adventures** tie-in novels (1991-97).

As of *Listen*, the concept of the Cartmel Masterplan can probably be considered to have been swept under the rug. Clara's few moments with the young Doctor show us something far less regal than the reincarnation that supposedly sprang from the genetic looms: a child, frightened of the dark, who had neither the wit nor the mettle to make it through the Academy. (For what it's worth, the 'wit' part holds true for much of what we know of the Doctor, given his 51% passing grade after multiple tries[54].)

We have always known, at least to some degree, that the Doctor is very wise, but not necessarily applied or studious. Incarnations like the third and the 12th are most definitely book-smart, but that's not necessarily a trait that persists across regenerations. What does remain is that, regardless of his intelligence, the Doctor's curiosity and desire for adventure will always reign supreme.

---

[53] It doesn't do to discuss the Masterplan here as it ended up influencing little of the 21st century series, but for the curious: the Doctor is a reincarnation of the Other, the third member of the Triumvirate that created the Time Lord class.
[54] *The Ribos Operation* (1978).

As for the 'scared' element, this has been revisited numerous times throughout the 21st century series. The Doctor always seems to be running in the show itself – but both Davies and Moffat turned that observation into a truth. Their Doctor runs. He's **on** the run. Because there are things he's afraid of. And one of those things may well be himself.

The Doctor, despite appearances at some times, does have rules for how he will engage with a problem. He has a playbook and will either refer to it or (at especially worrisome times) throw it out entirely. The Time Lord Victorious of *The Waters of Mars* (2009), as well as the reality-shattering actions of *Hell Bent*, remind us that the Doctor is well aware of what being a Time Lord affords him. And, on occasion, he falls victim to wanting to use that.

In *Death in Heaven* (2014), we see Missy offering the Doctor an army of Cybermen. The Master, arguably, knows the Doctor better than anyone, so Missy's offer would more than likely be relatively on the nose. She knows, as she keeps wanting to demonstrate during her Michelle Gomez incarnation, that she and the Doctor are not all that different. The Master may historically have extremely ridiculous plans, and her two most violent as Missy – giving the Doctor a Cyberman army and nearly walking him into killing his own companion out of rage[55] – seem especially over the top. But where the Master's previous plans have been world domination, Missy is solely focused on winning over the Doctor with logic. Thus, it stands to reason that she knows that her plans **have the potential to work.**

This puts us in a bind, because now we're in the position of discussing

---

[55] *The Witch's Familiar.*

that it is within the Doctor's character to do things that it's **not** within the Doctor's character to do. To clarify, it's possible for the Doctor **the person** to fall prey to these temptations – things that would not be done 'in the name of the Doctor.' For ease of discussion, let's separate the persona of the Doctor, the ideal that the War Doctor shed in order to end the Time War, from the Time Lord who chose the name. Lacking the Doctor's true name, let's fall back on his Academy nickname, Theta Sigma[56].

So where does Theta Sigma end and the Doctor begin? What things are inherently different about the two of them? And what causes Theta Sigma to drop the 'Doctor' persona?.

The Doctor

It's exceptionally difficult to do a perfect summing-up of the Doctor as a hero, but we do have a good effort from script editor Terrance Dicks:

> 'He never gives in, and he never gives up, however overwhelming the odds against him.
>
> 'The Doctor believes in good and fights evil. Though often caught up in violent situations, he is a man of peace. He is never cruel or cowardly'[57].

'Never cruel or cowardly' is repeated from one end of Steven

---

[56] First revealed in *The Armageddon Factor* (1979). It's not ideal, but it is safe to assume that the Doctor probably wasn't calling himself 'The Doctor' at the Academy.

[57] Dicks, Terrance, and Malcolm Hulke, *The Making of Doctor Who* (1976), p23.

Moffat's **Doctor Who** broadcast work[58] to the other[59], and it's certainly something that's held true across every change. There are times when the Doctor has been content to call himself a coward rather than a killer[60], but only when the other option is clearly a malevolent one.

While we may have these statements embedded in the series, there isn't a true 'rule book' when it comes to being the Doctor. In truth, the Doctor Rulebook exists only inside the Doctor's head. We can make several guesses as to what the Doctor's morals entail, simply given what we see of his actions throughout the last half century.

The Doctor favours peace. It is fair to say the Doctor abhors violence, but not to say he rejects it entirely. He has been known to handle a gun on some occasions when acting 'in the name of the Doctor,' but never to particularly enjoy it[61].

The Doctor believes in the sanctity of life across the universe – at one point even doubting his right to obliterate the Daleks before they are created[62]. The Doctor casts an especially kindly eye toward Earth, but will still force humans – his own Earthling companions included – to consider the rights of non-human species[63].

The Doctor's interventions in the Web of Time are not to make things

---

[58] *The Curse of Fatal Death* (1999).
[59] *Twice Upon a Time*.
[60] *The Parting of the Ways* (2005).
[61] In *The End of Time* (2010), we see him reject a service revolver from Wilf repeatedly until being told that Rassilon is back.
[62] *Genesis of the Daleks* (1975).
[63] Too many cases to mention – in the 12th Doctor's run alone we see this in *Kill the Moon*, *Smile*, and *Thin Ice* (2017), to name just three.

good, but to keep them as they are meant to be. He talks heavily of 'fixed points,' things that cannot be changed regardless of their fairness. The Doctor never uses time-travel powers to 'fix' set historical events that, if eliminated, could potentially alter the course of history, even positively[64].

In short, the Doctor acts altruistically, fairly, and kindly, in a way that preserves the natural order while still protecting the greatest number of people possible and routing away enemies who would make things otherwise.

Even without this breakdown, a new viewer to any era of **Doctor Who** could pick up this motivation pretty quickly. It makes up the core of the show, and it is our hero's driving motivation 99 times out of 100. But throughout series 9 of the 21st-century series – culminating in the actions of *Heaven Sent* and *Hell Bent* – we begin to see a very different person emerge. And through examination of this other side of the Doctor that emerges, we may get to know Theta Sigma, the Academy student who created the 'Doctor' persona.

Clothes Make the Man

Many of Peter Capaldi's costume choices during his run – from his 'Thin White Duke' ensemble[65] to his sonic sunglasses – existed notably to make pretending to be **Doctor Who** on the playground easier for younger children. *Listen* was our first vague step away from

---

[64] *Let's Kill Hitler* (2011), notably, but *Rose* (2005) notes his presence aboard the *Titanic* and at the assassination of JFK.
[65] The tidier look of Series 8 with waistcoat and collared shirt, named so here for its evocation of the David Bowie character of the same name.

the starched shirt look, with *Last Christmas* (2014) integrating a hoodie. By series 9, the Doctor had largely discarded the 'Rebel Time Lord'[66] aesthetic (minus the Crombie coat) in favour of T-shirts, hoodies, and jumpers.

One could potentially argue that the frequent costume changes were for marketing purposes, so that the BBC could turn out as many action figures as possible. But considering how few action figure variants were made, this is rather unlikely. Thus, we can connect it to the plot with little fear of misinterpretation.

The first true dress-down happens in *Listen*, when the Doctor is away from Clara as she's attempting to go on a date with Danny. This ties back in to his 'night-blogger' moments and his over-the-top curiosity – times when he's being less like the Doctor and more like the frightened child in the barn. Perhaps it's an early clue: the less Doctory the outfit, the less Doctory the Doctor.

Starting in *Last Christmas* and carrying over to the series 9 intro and its prequel, we see a Doctor very changed: he still flies the TARDIS, he still abides largely by his own rules, but he's got a look about him as though he's just rolled out of bed, rather than put himself together to look like the smartest person in the room. The Crombie coat and Loakes hold the look together, so he hasn't gone completely off the deep end. But there's something very 'day off' about the Doctor's look. As though he's just remembered he has to go in for a day of

---

[66] Gee, Catherine, 'First picture of Peter Capaldi's *Doctor Who* costume revealed.' Capaldi's own quote issued with the first image of the 12th Doctor in costume (albeit in the cardigan we would see only briefly): 'No frills, no scarf, no messing, just 100% Rebel Time Lord.'

Doctoring at the office and just put his nametag on top of his pyjamas.

This is also the series where we begin to see the Doctor's rules falter a bit. He has always loved his companions, and he has more than once had moments where their interest (or his in them) has come before that of the rest of the universe[67]. But series 9 sees a Doctor much more ready to say and do things to this extent. His and Clara's repeated confessions – direct or indirect – that they are an intrinsic part of each other's lives[68] seems to outweigh every instance of the Doctor being 'just a hobby' for Clara, or Clara being any less important to the Doctor than she ever was.

The Doctor presented to us is still the Doctor, true – he still saves the day, he still fights for what's right. But his constant underlying fear of abandonment, his odd 'softness' as compared to his starched shirt and short hair of Series 8, meshes with these sudden bouts of honesty and motivations based in the fear of losing Clara. We're not seeing a completely 'unmade' Doctor, but we're seeing him lapse the tiniest bit. As we see him throw on his trademark red-lined jacket over laundry day attire, we see him being Just Doctor Enough.

(It's important to note that this is not a critique of the writing. A character acting 'against type' does not always mean the writer doesn't understand them. The 12th Doctor's journey has heavy

---

[67] The 10th Doctor 'burning up a sun to say goodbye' in *Doomsday* (2006) comes to mind.
[68] The entirety of *Under the Lake / Before the Flood* (2015) hinges on this stipulation, and the Doctor's decision to leave Ashildr with a second immortality device in *The Girl Who Died* (2015) comes with a vague confession.

tones of self-discovery all through it, played out in different stages every series and right up into his final words in *Twice Upon a Time* (2017). If anything, seeing a finale like *Heaven Sent / Hell Bent*, bolstered so heavily by imagery played out throughout the show, reinforces that the move away from 'Doctorishness' comes both with awareness and with intent.)

It's appropriate, then, that when the Doctor is called out for a job by Riggsy in *Face the Raven*, he dresses up for it. This is the first time in quite a while that he is being specifically 'hired' for his services. This also readies him for his time in the Confession Dial – and throughout his multiple runs, he is the Doctor from head to toe.

At least, he seems to be.

Nothing Without an Audience

In *The Curse of Fatal Death* (1999) – not part of the TV series proper, but a piece of television that allows us to see what a pre-showrunner Moffat thought of the series – companion Emma snaps at Rowan Atkinson's Doctor and Jonathan Pryce's Master to 'stop showing off.' It's a silly throwaway line, but one that is later echoed much more firmly by the 11th Doctor: 'I'm being extremely clever up here and there's no one to stand around looking impressed! What's the point in having you all?'[69]

There's little to no secret that the Doctor benefits hugely from being observed. 'I'm nothing without an audience,' he tells us in *Heaven Sent*, throwing all of us at home a quick glance. It's a nod to his occasional (and occasionally quite understandable) arrogance. But

---

[69] *The Impossible Astronaut* (2011).

there's another side to this as well.

In *The Angels Take Manhattan* (2012), River Song begs the Doctor not to travel alone. We see, occasionally, what happens when he does so[70]. Without an observer – a 'carer,' in this Doctor's own words[71] – he is prone to being... well, less the Doctor.

So now we come to the storm room, the one room left out of the first chapter. It's an imagined TARDIS, of course, a place outside time and space where the Doctor can retreat to for daring escapes. While Jung never said anything about a TARDIS, applying his philosophy to this isn't difficult. The TARDIS is the Doctor's home. Specifically, it is the home of the **persona** known as the Doctor. It is the safe, secure place that can withstand any attack, launch off to any point in history, and cure any ill. It is the great problem-solver (and occasionally problem-finder).

So of course the Doctor would retreat to this 'mind palace' (to quote from a sister show[72]) to make his Doctory plans. Except... there's a big problem.

What the Doctor is doing, by definition, is not particularly Doctory at all.

We have no way of knowing this in *Heaven Sent*. It's a single-hander, after all. We have no companion save for the imaginary Clara, and only the Doctor to follow. And on a very real level, we are **in the Doctor's world**. Everything we see was created for, about, and

---

[70] Yet again in *Listen*, when he's at his maddest, Clara's first question is how long he's been alone.
[71] *Into the Dalek*.
[72] Steven Moffat and Mark Gatiss' **Sherlock** (2010-).

occasionally by him. This isn't a world at war or our own planet. This is the Doctor's struggle, inside and outside, and we're alone with him.

As we heard in *Face the Raven*, that's not necessarily a good thing.

Without context, the story of *Heaven Sent* is that the Doctor is trapped by the people who caused the death of his companion. They want something from him, and they are going to exploit him in any way possible to get it. Whoever they are, he hates them. And he will fight to keep this Great Secret to himself, sacrificing himself over and over for a chance to put things right.

He's a hero. But we have no one's point of view except his.

With the context of *Hell Bent*, we see the full picture: the truth he was hiding wasn't as huge or devastating as anyone believed. Clara, given the opportunity to speak, doesn't want saving[73]. The Doctor's 4,5000,000,000-year plan, previously awe-inspiring and tear-jerking, now carries the taint of selfishness.

Why, then, do we see Theta Sigma dressed as the Doctor, in the Doctor's TARDIS, talking to the Doctor's companion?

Because we're not the ones he needs to convince of what he's doing.

Theta Sigma

It takes some work to figure out the truth of the person behind the Doctor. A bad student? Yes. A scared child? Yes. But there is a great deal more to the nameless Time Lord than that.

---

[73] Again, she expressed her desires perfectly well in *Face the Raven*, but that didn't go too well.

As mentioned before, Missy tempts him multiple times. We can chalk up her actions to typical ridiculous Master plans, but – also as mentioned before – she knows her best friend better than anyone. Why give him a birthday present of an army if she knew he'd reject it? Why tempt him if he wouldn't be tempted?

The Doctor we know – the Doctor who asked, 'Have I the right?' in the face of destroying the Daleks – would not be tempted by her gifts. But she's not trying to tempt the Doctor. She's aiming for the person underneath the name. The person who **would** accept power to make the universe the way he thinks it should be.

It would be incorrect to call Theta Sigma a 'bad person.' Because while the Doctor has done some things that would not fly in court[74], he has overall remained above the 'neutral' line of the alignment chart[75]. As mentioned before, he also spends the entire of Series 8 genuinely concerned about his goodness, and inevitably concludes in *Death in Heaven* that he is 'an idiot,' neither good nor bad.

This brings up another important point, and one exercised a great deal in the Moffat era but also in Series 8 specifically: the character's deep-seated self-loathing. In *Time Heist* (2014), we hear this quite clearly: 'He's overbearing, he's manipulative, he likes to think he's very clever.' Elements that the Doctor hates about himself, manifested in another persona (the episode's 'Architect'), which eventually allows him to figure out that he himself is the individual

---

[74] Literally (*The Trial of a Time Lord*).
[75] Alternate personas, like the aforementioned serial's Valeyard or the Dream Lord of *Amy's Choice*, may be a bit harder to peg. But they are deliberately twisted manifestations of the Doctor, not the individual exerting any sort of regular agency.

he loathes so much.

A similar revelation comes about in *Amy's Choice* (2010), as the Dream Lord is revealed to be the person the Doctor most hates in the universe. Short answer? Himself.

These moments tell us one of the deepest, most important things we need to understand about Theta Sigma: **this person hates himself**. He understand his propensity for being extremely manipulative to get what he wants. he knows his the capacity to do terrible (or terrible-seeming) things in the name of 'doing right.' And he dislikes that about himself immensely.

A person like that – with potentially harmful faults and an acute awareness of them, yet a strong desire to help nonetheless – would need to keep himself in check. 'To hold [himself] to the mark,' as it were[76]. That set of rules, that restraint, is the Doctor. Not the person, but the 'costume' he puts on, to shove the manipulative know-it-all to the back of the frame so that he can actually do the good he wants to see.

The Unreliable Narrator

Confession in a religious sense is, despite the ritual, a deeply personal and contemplative thing – especially before death, which is when we are told the Confession Dials of the Time Lords are meant to be used[77]. The Doctor's may have been converted into something of an interrogation room, but its build still betrays it as something

---

[76] The Doctor in *The Girl Who Died*, subconsciously giving himself a reminder of what it is he's meant to do.

[77] *The Magician's Apprentice*.

meant for the individual.

He is, after all, alone with himself on a very real level. His 'enemy' is a memory he himself created. He even constitutes the dust and skulls filling the castle. And, as mentioned before, the gear imagery (on a metatextual level) ties us back to the visuals of the opening sequence and this Doctor's very specific nature.

Why, then, the TARDIS as a storm room? Why the Doctory clothes? Why the Doctorish patter, jokes, and problem-solving? Perhaps it's a feeling of being watched – of being unsure, on some level, whether he is being observed, and wanting to keep the heroic image strong in case his enemies are keeping an eye on him. Perhaps it's a fear tactic, reverting to his 'stronger self' to make sure he gets out in one piece and doesn't lose hope.

But we've seen the Doctor alone before. Not just this version, but many others. We know what they're like in the absence of an audience. Sometimes angry, sometimes contemplative, often simply afraid. The Doctor of recent years has no trouble, provided he's alone, admitting he's afraid[78]. And this Doctor in particular, when completely alone, tends to soliloquise, panic, and overthink[79].

It's possible he's showboating for an unseen enemy, of course, as evidenced by his repeated monologue as he steps out of the 'teleporter.' But there's far more reason to believe that the Doctor persona is for the benefit of himself... not because of fear, but to justify his actions to himself.

---

[78] *Hide* (2013), and *Heaven Sent* itself.
[79] Once again, *Listen*. An excellent episode to go back to for laying the 12th Doctor's personality bare, long before *Heaven Sent*.

Clara is, throughout her run with the 12th Doctor, his grounding influence. She reconnects him to humans after his superficial humanity seems to escape him somewhat with his new regeneration cycle[80]. She teaches him to 'interface' respectfully with people, to make the right decisions at difficult times. She reminds him, whether actively or passively, what he's fighting for.

And yet, when she appears in the storm room, her face is to the wall in all but one instance of speaking to her.

This could be for artistic purposes, of course. It could be a foreshadowing of the Doctor's neural block in *Hell Bent*, or a call-back to turning mirrors and portraits toward the wall in the case of a death. But considering he couldn't bear to turn **his** portrait of her away, it seems odd that in his own mental sanctuary, his primary source of comfort would lack a face.

We hit upon a moment in the life of both Theta Sigma the person and the Doctor the character when the two intersect on a very different level. In the past, the Doctor's 'Time Lord Victorious' acts have been far grander, far more frightening. But here, we see our hero fighting for his life, sacrificing himself over and over for freedom. We see him near death, dying, mourning his own position, mourning his solitude, and wanting to give up. And then we see him regain his strength to punch through the wall.

Prior to *Hell Bent*, the summary of *Heaven Sent* is quite different. On its own, it's the story of the Doctor overcoming an unseen enemy to free himself and exact justice on the people who, in order to get their

---

[80] *The Time of the Doctor.*

hands on him, inadvertently killed Clara.

But after *Hell Bent*, it is the story of a man with a plan, so bent on revenge that he's willing to burn himself alive for billions of years just to see it come to pass, instead of uttering what would ultimately be some harmless words.

We can't know for sure if or when the Doctor became aware that the murder castle was his Confession Dial. He's a smart guy, so we can guess that he may have come to this conclusion after examining all the facts in front of him. He shows little trace of surprise when he finds himself on Gallifrey at the end of the episode, and his engine already seems to be revved up to kick into Revenge Mode. His mind works in split seconds, yes, but there's a difference between escaping a trap in front of you and bringing down a planet.

So if the Doctor knew he was in his Confession Dial, if he knew he was essentially alone, and he knew he was 'hell bent' on revenge, who was the Doctor acting for?

The only person there: himself.

Be a Doctor

It wouldn't be fair to say the Doctor wants to be a bad person. He may have a rap sheet as long as your arm, including everything from kidnapping to attempted murder to passive genocide, but moral grey in action is not the same as a lack of desire to be an upstanding person. Yes, he came to the resolution that he is not a bad person – that he's an idiot and he's doing his best; probably the fairest assessment anyone could grant him. But doing the rightest thing possible is still foremost in his mind.

There is no way a man who questioned his right to destroy the Daleks and offers second chances to even the worst of people **wouldn't** know that abusing his top-tier Time Lord powers to rescue Clara is not a Doctory thing to do.

Toward the end of the 10th Doctor's run, we see a similar lapse in judgment[81]. However, in his earlier 'Time Lord Victorious' mode, he invokes superiority over the laws of time for what he sees as a greater good, rather than keeping a friend alive. We see him veering in a similar direction in *Hell Bent* – when he has discarded his Doctory look together to go 'as close to Shane as we dare'[82] – with disastrous results. But prior to this, prior to our Theta Sigma going **literally** Wild West on us, there is a deep and deliberate attempt to remain as much the Doctor as possible.

Theta Sigma knows. No matter how bad his grades were at the Academy, he knows. And we know. It's generally frowned upon to rip apart time and space and jerk someone out of their timeline, potentially shattering the very fabric of the universe, just for the sake of that one person. The Doctor, the persona, **absolutely** knows. And the Doctor would stop anyone else who tried to do this. The only way to resolve the two halves of this dilemma is for Theta Sigma to 'play Doctor' to the hilt as he prepares to do something that the deepest and most essential aspects of the persona would never allow him to do.

His audience is **him. He** is the one he must convince. And provided he can make himself believe that the Doctor would be completely

---

81 *The Waters of Mars.*

82 Moffat, Steven, '**Doctor Who** Series 9 Episode 12 *Hell Bent*: Green Amendments', p11.

okay with this, then he can go through with it.

And in doing this, he has fooled his unexpected, constant audience – us, the extension of the companion – just as fully.

It's why we can latch on to the sentiment of his actions even while understanding the actual negative aspects of them. He's deliberately altering the script (or at least his and our perception of it), allowing himself to play the hero while gearing up to do something that is ultimately quite selfish.

Basically, It's the Eyebrows

Returning again to the topic of Missy – notably present in the series 9 opener rather than its finale – she remains, even into series 10, the one person who can truly give us a good read on Theta Sigma wearing the Doctor's clothes. She understands both the person and the persona he's trying to be.

'Your version of good is not absolute,' she points out to him as he is attempting to rehabilitate her. 'It's vain, arrogant, and sentimental.'[83] Missy, more than anyone – more than even the Doctor himself, at times – seems the most capable of evaluating her childhood friend as a whole individual. She recognises the Doctor persona as something that was ultimately his creation.

We talked in a previous chapter about how the Confession Dial, like a computer program, can only operate within its programming; that any creation is inherently impeded by the intelligence and morality of its creator. So too with the persona of the Doctor: despite the fact that it exists as Theta Sigma's way to 'be good' and 'do right,' it is still

---

[83] *The Lie of the Land* (2017).

a character from the mind of an individual with his own morality. Thus, the Doctor can never be objectively **good**. He have moments of questioning this, other moments when he becomes all right with it, but still many, many pitfalls (both as the 12th and in other incarnations) when he puts himself forward as the authority because... well. The Doctor exists to be good and just, therefore goodness and justice should have the floor.

It is this very mentality that makes it easy for Theta Sigma, for 'the Doctor,' to fool himself as he enacts his plan. At his most sincere, he acknowledges that he is fallible. At his most motivated, he cannot be. And with morality not truly a part of the puzzle within the Confession Dial – with it being simply a trap he must get out of rather than a moral conundrum he must solve – he is free to **Win!**

The False Clara

And finally, we go back to Clara Oswald. Because in series 9, the pairing of the Doctor and Clara is the 'same old, same old'[84]. Without her, he would potentially have alienated every person he tried to save. He wouldn't have grown as much as he did – he would have grown, yes, but it would have been much harder. In essence, her presence is as much a part of his Doctor 'costume' as the Doctory jacket or the fancy spaceship.

Or rather, that's how it is **in his mind**. Remember that her continued presence has caused him to drop his 'uniform,' to act more like the bad schoolboy and less like the Old Man of Time. Which is not a knock against Clara the character; she spent her entire run teaching as best she could. And again, Missy knew what she was doing when

---

[84] *The Witch's Familiar.*

she found Clara – she knew what sort of person her old school friend would be most vulnerable to[85].

But Clara is so integrated that, even in her absence, he cannot go ahead without her approval. Thus, he creates a false Clara. One that, interestingly, never says anything particularly specific about his plans, save that he's got to 'win' – which makes a degree of sense. If she is as imprinted on his hearts and mind as he claims in *The Zygon Inversion*, it's highly unlikely that he could persuade even a mental construct of her to approve of something he knows she would dislike. But Clara would want the Doctor to fight and win, and for his purposes, that's enough.

So, with *Heaven Sent* fairly picked apart, what are we left with? A bad student who made up his own superhero identity, and is using it to trick himself into doing some morally-grey stuff to get his girl back while the universe falls apart around them. And someone has trapped him in a castle that is designed from the ground up to get something very specific out of him.

From within the story, that's a single line of information. But on a metatextual level, the Confession Dial is a perfectly oiled and calibrated Character Development Machine.

---

[85] *Death in Heaven.*

CHAPTER 5: ENDLESS TWELVE

The use of temporal loops in fiction can be an extremely powerful – and thoroughly mind-boggling – narrative tool. Handled poorly, they can become irritating and trite. But applied to the right story and the right character, they serve the writer well for suspense, horror, or character development.

In a very basic way, it's a metaphor for 'spinning one's wheels,' though rarely is the loop itself ever so benign or boring. The repetition adds a level of uncanniness and fear to the experience – where one would simply slog through day after day of similar work activities, realising it's always the exact same date is another matter entirely. It adds a level of urgency, a need to escape.

The primary focus of the temporal loop is, of course, how one gets out of it (or **if** one gets out of it). The breaking of the loop signifies the development or discovery the character was in need of. In other words, the loop can only break once the character has learned their lesson.

Hell Is Repetition

In the endnotes to his 1998 short story 'That Feeling, You Can Only Say What It Is in French,' horror writer Stephen King is quoted as saying, 'There's an idea that hell is other people. My idea is that it might be repetition.' He makes good use of this in two of his fictional works. The first, the aforementioned short story, takes the statement quite literally. Originally published in *The New Yorker*, it follows Carol on her second honeymoon with her good-enough-but-not-great husband Bill. She keeps predicting – at least to a very close degree – what will be coming next on the road in front of them as they drive, only to be cut off with the same terrifying words and imagery. The implication at the end of the story is that the pair died in a plane crash, and are now doomed to relive the moment over and over.

King's story invokes a skipping-rope rhyme – 'Hey there, Mary, what's the story / Save my ass from Purgatory.' The implication could be, then, that Carol and Bill are not in Hell, but rather 'burning off' their various sins[86]. Still, the story ends with no ending in sight, and with a distinct sense of despair from Carol.

The second is *The Dark Tower* (2004), the finale to King's **Dark Tower** series, in which interdimensional cowboy Roland Deschain goes to see the eponymous structure (and perhaps save all of existence along the way if the mood takes him). King prefaces his big reveal with a note to his readers, saying that the story ends with Roland's arrival at the Tower, and that we can read on if we desire but we probably won't like it. The story's true end reveals the Tower's top door to be a gateway to the wasteland of the first book, *The Gunslinger* (1982), dragging Roland back into his journey once again. As with Carol, the moment comes when Roland realises what he's been doing all this time and what he's about to be drawn back into.

Unlike Carol, however, he now finds himself possessed of the Horn of Eld: an artefact that he was notably missing during the series. We are given to believe that its presence could have helped Roland avoid some tragedies for which he's still burning off a great deal of guilt – impossible to list here in a book about another franchise entirely, but

---

[86] Bill's affair with an assistant, for one. Another is potentially Carol's abortion, which is swept under the rug by her extremely Catholic family. We get the feeling there may be many more we're missing.

notably weighty, diverse, and terrible.

We are not with either of King's protagonists for the closing of their loops[87]. Rather, the climax of their story comes at the realisation that a loop exists. Thus, the loop exists for horror – a promise of future character development when we are long gone from these characters' lives, perhaps, but mainly for a horrified reaction.

Rather pleasingly, the Doctor's revelation doesn't necessarily come alongside the viewers' in *Heaven Sent*. An astute fan could pick up the concept of the loop with the Doctor's observation of the stars, or the juxtaposition of one of the skulls and the Doctor's face, or the dry clothes waiting over the chair by the fire. A reveal does still occur, but much of its impact is reliant upon when a viewer knows. Guessing before the Doctor can be painful; finding out along with him is more a quiet, sad reflection.

It wouldn't be true to say that the revelation of the temporal loop doesn't exist to induce some degree of horror, just because it's broken. As mentioned before, the loop is almost certainly a function of the castle. The castle exists to create enough despair to get the Doctor to give over what he knows. It's a handy way to give the audience a deep degree of unease at the same time.

Eternal Summer

The unease, fear, and exhaustion of a temporal loop can be one of

---

[87] Except potentially for Roland, as early advertising for the *Dark Tower* film adaptation notably featured the Horn of Eld and text reading 'LAST TIME AROUND'. At the time of this writing, the future of the planned **Dark Tower** franchise is uncertain, so anything further on whether this really is Roland's 'last time around' will have to wait.

the most difficult things to convey in a limited space of entertainment. The short story 'Endless Eight', featured in Nagaru Tanigawa's light novel *The Rampage of Haruhi Suzumiya* (2004), presented a single iteration – the final one, to be specific – of a two-week loop. We see four members of a high school's paranormal adventuring club reliving their summer vacation over 15,000 times because their president – an easily bored girl who is unaware of her godlike powers – is dissatisfied with how her time is spent. The exhaustion of the repetition is manifested in Yuki, a humanoid computer who is unaffected by the loop's 'reset' and remembers every repetition perfectly.

When the story was adapted for the light novel series' anime run, the tactics were much more vicious. Eight 'Endless Eight' episodes were produced and aired one after the other during the show's second season. Each episode was re-scripted, re-storyboarded, re-voiced, and re-animated. The audience was given no indication of how long the arc would run, with fan sites and messageboards exploding in anger whenever the episode of the week opened with the narrator uttering the phrase 'Something's wrong.' Maddening at the time, the structure was genius in retrospect – and perhaps the only way to accurately put the audience through the same weariness that the characters experienced.

As with the previous examples, *Heaven Sent* explores primarily a single slice of the loop: one repetition approximately 7,000 years in. In that respect, the majority of it has more in common with King's *The Dark Tower*, where our primary journey is discovering that the loop exists.

However, when called upon to convey the weariness and

neverending nature of the 12th Doctor's loop, Moffat and Talalay have gone the exact opposite direction from 'Endless Eight': rather than stretching the story out with no end in sight, they wheel out a breathless montage, repetition upon repetition, driving home the endless nature of the Doctor's predicament as the years and skulls stack up.

While that element of the time loop does lend another shade of horror to the story, it's a very notable decision to make the audience feel it, too – to not only terrify them with its existence, but to make the predicament felt.

It's Cold Out There

In the modern era, Harold Ramis' 1993 romance-drama *Groundhog Day* has made its mark in the zeitgeist as The Time Loop Story. Even Syfy's TV adaptation of **12 Monkeys** (2015-18) sees a character quote-checking the film when the cast are stuck in a temporal loop of their own[88].

There is, however, an excellent reason for its staying power. This film, more than any other major title, has perfected the use of the temporal loop as a character development mechanism. Bill Murray's Phil remembers every iteration of the loop. His reactions run the gamut of a character in need of redemption at first, from attempts at making the system work for him to outright suicide. It isn't until he turns his misfortune into an advantage – using his time to improve himself – that he finds his way out and can move forward with his life.

---

[88] **12 Monkeys:** *Lullaby* (2016).

As with King's two works, we see a concept of temporal loops as purgatorial: perfectly in line with the Confession Dial of the Time Lords. And in a modern context, one cannot invoke a temporal loop without invoking *Groundhog Day* to some degree – even if only as a thought in the back of someone's mind. Therefore, the simple act of involving the plot device in one's story brings to mind redemption and self-assessment.

Tailor-Made

On the far side of this monograph, we have a fairly tall pile of evidence that the Confession Dial is more than just a bespoke torture chamber – on a metatextual level, at least.

Let us step outside the confines of the narrative of the moment and examine the episode itself from all angles. The 12th Doctor is the first new Doctor of the series' second half-century – paired with Clara, a companion who evokes the link between the two eras of the series in multiple ways[89]. His choice of face is a reminder to himself to be the Doctor[90]. Of all the Doctors, despite his prickly exterior, he is the one who most wears his heart on his sleeve. His run, from beginning to end, was one of self-discovery, self-assessment, and defining solidly what makes the Doctor the Doctor. More than ever, we saw the line between the Doctor and the Time Lord who played that role

---

[89] Her presence in *The Day of the Doctor*, her role in *The Name of the Doctor* when she fractures across his timelines, etc. Even her name is a nod to the middle name of beloved 20th-century companion actor Elisabeth Sladen.
[90] *The Girl Who Died*.

drawn sharply, and knowingly stepped over on multiple occasions[91]. The person lost sight of the persona – the driving force of the series and his adventures – in his dedication to a companion, despite that companion's insistence that he hold to that persona.

And now, he's taken away and dropped into a castle made for him. The structure is modelled on top of a classic blueprint for psychological self-examination. Its gears turn with truth, and its walls move with discovery. It separates the Doctor from his audience so that he is alone with his persona. And all of this is wrapped up in a literary trope that exists to produce growth.

In other words – within the show's structure, the Confession Dial was built to trap the Doctor until he confessed. But in the world of the show, it was built to trap the Doctor until he experienced character growth. It is a literal Character Development Machine, so obviously perfect that it practically shouts it to the viewer.

And the Doctor decides he's not having it and punches his way out.

This active flight by a protagonist from his development is an intriguing one, because it's open to so many different readings. But for the purposes of this book, there are two specifically worth zooming in on: the Doctor resisting growth in his own life, and the more 'meta' resistance to him developing as a character within his own show.

In Search of an Exit

Being pushed into a corner and forced to self-observe and change –

---

[91] With the Doctor going so far as to tell Davros in *The Witch's Familiar* that 'the Doctor doesn't exist.'

81

be it by Time Lords or a showrunner – is not a comfortable spot for someone like the Doctor. He's always right, except for the times he quite nobly admits he's not. He always knows best. He is the Old Man of the Universe, with more experience and better judgment (allegedly) than anyone. And now, in the midst of a desire for revenge after being very specifically brought to heel by Clara[92], he's being stopped and forced to reflect and adjust. Will he be a Warrior? Or will he be a Doctor?

Or – the third option – will he be Theta Sigma, the self-assured Academy student who knows best in all things?

Should he choose anything but change – which, of course, he does – he will be forced back. It's not a matter of 'the easy way' and 'the hard way', so much as 'the hard way' and 'the really quite awful way.' But his choice, however heroic it seemed without context, will be undone by the time *Hell Bent* wraps. He will have to accept his loss. He will have to let Clara go. He will have to hold to the mark and become the Doctor once again.

'I Don't Want You to Change'

To begin to address fan complaint with the 21st century series is a dangerous road to go down, because every breath drawn by every crew member has a complaint attached to it somewhere. Some are valid, some are subjective, and some are just odd. One in particular that tends to surface, though, is the Doctor's change in characterisation after the 50th anniversary.

---

[92] 'You will not insult my memory. There will be no revenge.' (*Face the Raven*). A very clear request, but one that most viewers probably knew would go out the window shortly after.

A popular cry on social media has been the idea that the Doctor's character from 2005 to 2013 no longer matters since his Time War 'genocide' was undone in *The Day of the Doctor* (2013)[93]. Granted, many safeties were put in place to avoid this accusation: time bubbles, carefully timed memory lapses, and the like[94]. But the complaints ring: since he is no longer a killer, and since Gallifrey still exists, has Russell T Davies' era not effectively been undone? Have the Doctor's grief, growth, and change during that time been pointless?

The extraction of Gallifrey from 21st-century **Doctor Who** was done primarily for storytelling purposes: the Time Lords' constant presence, according to regular writer Mark Gatiss, makes them appear 'domesticated' and 'like a bunch of MPs' with overuse[95]. Whether it was 'right' to bring them back will likely never be decided with any level of objectivity, and the playing field could very easily

---

[93] A lasting example is Tumblr user linnealurks asking Robert Shearman for his take on this, and the thread that followed: 'Have you watched *The Day of the Doctor*, and if so (and if diplomacy permits), do you have any comments? A lot of people are very annoyed with the way it retcons a fundamental part of Nine's and Ten's character arcs. I for one am going to pretend it never happened.'

[94] In *The Day of the Doctor*; it's heavily implied that the Doctor will continue to believe he is a mass murderer until he reaches the relevant point in the 11th Doctor's timeline. Which makes sense: the War Doctor stealing and activating a superweapon, followed by missing time and a missing planet, will probably not register to him and his future regenerations as 'I didn't kill anyone, I just stowed it all in a painting at the last minute.'

[95] 'Gatiss on Gallifrey & Time Lords' Return'.

change yet again under new showrunner Chris Chibnall.

This, though, is simply the latest in the fanbase's resistance to change. Saying there has never been a push against any alteration made to the show – writer, actor, format, budget, mood – would be laughable. And in the 21st-century series, with writers and actors pulled from the highly experimental 'Wilderness Years,' changes come far more readily. This has alienated some viewers and enamoured others.

At the time of this book's writing, the Doctor has just regenerated into a woman for the first time in the show's 55-year history. Viewers' opinions, understandably, have been vocal in a variety of directions. Perhaps in a few decades someone will be baffled that such an uproar existed. But the 12th Doctor's status as the Doctor of both rediscovery and change came at a uniquely perfect time: a time when the audience is going through confusion of its own about what **Doctor Who** truly is.

The Doctor's resistance to reflection and change is almost certainly not Steven Moffat's coded message to the fanbase about how deeply set against change a large portion of it appears to be. That's far too deep a reading, even for a monograph of this nature. But the pairing of the sentiment with a Doctor meant to bring about pacing and mood changes with the series is not necessarily lost.

'And Be a Doctor'

Regardless, the Confession Dial does its work, both on a story level and on a metatextual level. Just not the way it was necessarily intended.

By the time series 10 rolls around, with two Christmas specials in between for the tying up of some loose ends and the introduction of one of two new companions, we do definitely see a changed 12th Doctor. He still embraces his casual wear[96]. He still plays his guitar when given the opportunity[97]. On the other hand, he's still always right except when he deems it proper to say he's not, and his morality continues to walk lines that even he isn't necessarily keen to straddle[98].

What we see in this Doctor's final series is a merging of those two sides of himself – the selfish, idealistic Academy student and the selfless do-gooder superhero. The dutiful Time Lord and the irresponsible adventurer. The teacher and the student.

The 12th Doctor of series 10 is a pile of contradictions, rejecting affection one moment and smiling childishly the next as he tells a new companion that the sky is made of lemon drops[99]. Leaving his closest associates out of his plan, and then bringing them back to the fold as if nothing happened. But he demonstrates that he has learned all the things that Clara hoped for him to learn – albeit in her absence.

And finally, in *Twice Upon a Time*, all his lessons come together as he looks both forwards and backwards. The rejected character

---

[96] While the Doctor does begin to expand his wardrobe of jackets, the hoodies and shirts still swap in.
[97] *The Pilot.*
[98] The finale of the series' central trilogy, *The Lie of the Land,* hinges in a large part on selective manipulation of the people closest to him. It is also, as mentioned earlier, the episode in which Missy makes it a point to call him out on his brand of morality.
[99] *The Pilot.*

development took some time to land; but when it did, it struck true, and served its purpose.

CHAPTER 6: FINAL THOUGHTS

I would never, in any of my readings of *Heaven Sent*, venture to say that any interpretation set forth is the 'right one.' Creatives involved with the production can state their reasoning behind certain choices, but even those work better as elements of discussion than a be-all and end-all. Despite a temptation to call Death of the Author and slap a Seal of Objectivity on the whole thing, it's actually far more fulfilling and interesting to allow all of this to be a great 'what if'.

Jungian readings of texts are on two levels. The first is the obvious: connecting symbols and applying Jung's psychology to the imagery. The second is less obvious, but more intriguing: the idea that a piece of symbolism can be true and right and still completely unintentional. The idea that symbolism is so ingrained in human nature that meaning will escape from our minds onto the page without us having even put them there in the first place.

Of all the televised **Doctor Who** writers of any era so far, Steven Moffat is the most 'literary' when it comes to his storytelling. Amelia Pond was the girl with the fairytale name, waiting for her mysterious imaginary friend. Clara Oswald was an English teacher whose greatest dream was to meet a fictional character. The 11th Doctor was an imaginary friend in a run of fairytale sensibilities, while the 12th went from coarse to soft to literally blinded like a tragic Gothic hero in a capital-R Romance. But all of the above are still styles of storytelling steeped in meaning and imagery.

To claim that Moffat invoked Jung's symbolic meaning of diamond or tapped into Middle Eastern funeral rites is not impossible, but also not a sure bet. The fact remains, though, that the imagery was present, and put together (intentionally or not) it creates a compelling second – or third or fourth – layer to the story already presented. The Death of the Author is not necessary to appreciate a potentially unintentional message. Just as writers have stories in their DNA, so do readers and listeners. And even if we don't completely latch on to what we're seeing and hearing, we see and hear it.

The most prominent stories of the 12th Doctor's run are stories of self-discovery – whether successful or subverted. His run is a wealth of riches for those seeking to understand the truth of the Doctor and the Time Lord who wears that name. And *Heaven Sent* remains high on that list: showing us a Doctor in the middle of his evolution, rejecting the inevitable but soon to rediscover what has made him who he is.

BIBLIOGRAPHY

Books

Dicks, Terrance, and Malcolm Hulke, *The Making of Doctor Who*. London, W H Allen, 1976. ISBN 9780426116158.

Jung, Carl, *Memories, Dreams, Reflections*. Richard and Clara Winston, trans, Hampton Falls, Grant, 1963. ISBN 9780394702681.

Jung, Carl, *Psychology and Alchemy*. RFC Hull, trans, Princeton, Princeton University Press, 1980. ISBN 9780691018317.

King, Stephen, *The Dark Tower*. New York City, Pantheon Books, 2004. ISBN 9781416524526.

Tanigawa, Nagaru, *The Rampage of Haruhi Suzumiya*. New York City, Yen Press, 2011. ISBN 9780316038843.

Periodicals

King, Stephen, 'That Feeling, You Can Only Say What It Is in French'. *The New Yorker* Summer Fiction issue, 22 and 29 June 1998.

Television

The Melancholy of Haruhi Suzumiya. Kyoto Animation, 2006-09.

   Endless Eight (eight episodes), 2009.

Twelve Monkeys. NBC Universal, 2015-18.

   Lullaby, 2016.

Film

Arcel, Nikolaj, dir, *The Dark Tower*. Columbia Pictures, 2017.

Derrickson, Scott, dir, *Dr Strange*. Marvel Studios, 2016.

Johnston, Joe, dir, *Jumanji*. Tristar Pictures, 1995.

Ramis, Harold, dir, *Groundhog Day*. Columbia Pictures, 1993.

Talalay, Rachel, dir, *Freddy's Dead: The Final Nightmare*. New Line Cinema, 1991.

Audio CD

Shearman, Rob, *Scherzo*. **Doctor Who**. Big Finish Productions, 2003.

Web

'Gatiss on Gallifrey & Time Lords' Return.' *Doctor Who TV,* 22 March 2014. http://www.doctorwhotv.co.uk/gatiss-on-gallifrey-time-lords-return-61906.htm. Accessed 17 August 2017.

Connolly, Kelly, 'Doctor Who Recap: *Heaven Sent.' Entertainment Weekly,* 29 Nov. 2015. http://ew.com/recap/doctor-who-season-9-episode-11/. Accessed 28 February 2018.

Fullerton, Huw, 'Steven Moffat Has Filled in the "Plot Holes" from **Doctor Who**: *Heaven Sent'*. RadioTimes.com http://www.radiotimes.com/news/2016-01-07/steven-moffat-has-filled-in-the-plot-holes-from-doctor-who-heaven-sent/. Accessed 10 June 2017.

Gee, Catherine, 'First picture of Peter Capaldi's *Doctor Who'* costume revealed.' *The Telegraph*, 27 January 2014. https://www.telegraph.co.uk/culture/tvandradio/doctor-who/10599910/First-picture-of-Peter-Capaldis-Doctor-Who-costume-revealed.html. Accessed 8 April 2018.

Grimm, Jacob and Wilhelm, 'The Shepherd Boy'. Grimms' Fairy Tales. https://www.grimmstories.com/en/grimm_fairy-tales/the_shepherd_boy. Accessed 26 May 2017.

Martin, Tim, '**Doctor Who**: *Heaven Sent* – Five Things We Learned, Plus the Return of River Song'. *The Telegraph*, 1 December 2015. https://www.telegraph.co.uk/culture/tvandradio/doctor-who/12017034/doctor-who-heaven-sent-what-time-recap-review-clara.html. Accessed 28 February 2018.

Moffat, Steven, '**Doctor Who** Series 9 Episode 12 *Heaven Sent*: Blue Amendments'. BBC Writers' Room. http://www.bbc.co.uk/writersroom/scripts/doctor-who-series-9. Accessed 12 August 2017.

Moffat, Steven, '**Doctor Who** Series 9 Episode 12 *Hell Bent*: Green Amendments'. BBC Writers' Room. http://www.bbc.co.uk/writersroom/scripts/doctor-who-series-9. Accessed 12 August 2017.

BIOGRAPHY

Kara Dennison is a writer, illustrator, interviewer, and presenter from Virginia. She discovered **Doctor Who** at the age of 18, and worked for four years as Community Manager for the Baltimore-area convention (Re)Generation Who. During her time with the event, she conducted several notable presentations, including Peter Capaldi's first public interview after leaving **Doctor Who**.

As a writer, Kara has appeared in the **Doctor Who** related titles *Seasons of War: Gallifrey*, *A Target for Tommy*, and *Nine Lives*. Her work has also been published in *The Perennial Miss Wildthyme*, two **City of the Saved** anthologies, *Ride the Star Wind*, *My American Nightmare*, and many others. Together with illustrator Ginger Hoesly, she is one of the creators of the light novel series **Owl's Flower**.

Kara works from a converted NASA shed with four guinea pigs, where she spends most of her time drinking tea and writing anime news. You can find her blogging for Crunchyroll and VRV, or continuing to overanalyse geek entertainment at karadennison.com.

Coming Soon

The Black Archive #22: Hell Bent by Alyssa Franke

The Black Archive #23: The Curse of Fenric by Una McCormack

The Black Archive #24: The Time Warrior by Matthew Kilburn

The Black Archive #25: Doctor Who (1996) by Paul Driscoll

The Black Archive #26: The Dæmons by Matt Barber

The Black Archive #27: The Face of Evil by Thomas Rodebaugh

The Black Archive #28: Love & Monsters by Niki Haringsma

The Black Archive #29: Warriors' Gate by Frank Collins

The Black Archive #30: Survival by Craig Jones

The Black Archive #31: The Impossible Astronaut / Day of the Moon by John Toon

The Black Archive #32: The Romans by Jacob Edwards